The Fathers on Christology

The Fathers

on

Christology

*THE DEVELOPMENT OF
CHRISTOLOGICAL DOGMA
FROM THE BIBLE TO
THE GREAT COUNCILS*

by P. SMULDERS, S.J.

Translated by LUCIEN ROY, S.J.

ST. NORBERT ABBEY PRESS
De Pere, Wisconsin
U. S. A.
1968

Edited by Lisa McGaw

Translation: International Publishing Consultants
Amsterdam, the Netherlands

Cover design: Patricia Ellen Ricci

© 1968 St. Norbert Abbey Press

Standard Book Number 8316-1051-4

Library of Congress Catalogue Number 68-58125

Printed in the United States of America
ST. NORBERT ABBEY PRESS
De Pere, Wisconsin 54115

CONTENTS

INTRODUCTION[*]

In Bologna on the titular feast of a convent where his sister was abbess, Pope Benedict XIV celebrated the Pontifical High Mass. The nuns had practiced their most beautiful Mass and in the sung Creed the words "begotten not made" were repeated in endless variations. Irritated by this warbling, the Pope turned around in the middle of their singing and in a deep voice chanted: "Begotten or made, the peace of the Lord be always with you." Then he began the Offertory. Döllinger, the church historian, shared this anecdote with the Protestant theologian A. Ritschl, who was delighted at this expression of papal relativism.[1]

A tendency toward a certain relativism can easily

*At the request of the editors of this journal we are publishing here a summary review of the development of christological dogma, which was written in the framework of a correspondence course about Christology prepared by the Nederlands Schriftelijk Studiecentrum. These lessons in the hisory of dogma were preceded by studies concerning the Christology of the New Testament and followed by a treatment of the Scholastic teaching of Christology and redemption. The lessons were printed without any alterations, which thus accounts for certain lacunae, especially in the biblical foundation of our study.

overcome us when we read the great christological dogmas. The essential formulae are familiar:

The **Council of Nicaea** (325):

> We believe . . . in one Lord Jesus Christ, the Son of God, as the only-begotten Son of the Father, that is from the substance of the Father, God from God, light from light, true God from true God, begotten not made, of one substance with the Father, through whom all things were made. . . . He came down for us men and became incarnate and was made man, suffered and on the third day rose (H. Denzinger—A. Schönmetzer, **Enchiridion Symbolorum**, Editio XXXIV [Herder, 1967], no. 125). [This work will be cited henceforth as **DS**.]

The **First Council of Constantinople** (381) condemned Apollinaris. The liturgical confession of faith which we use in the Creed originated in the circumstances of this Council.

The **Council of Ephesus** (431) condemned Nestorius and his proposition that Mary is not actually the Mother of God but only the Mother of Christ, as being opposed to the teaching of Nicaea. This Council promulgated no new dogmatic formula but attached its highest approbation to the second letter of Cyril to Nestorius,[2] in which the faith of Nicaea was set forth as follows:

> We do not profess that the nature of the Word

became flesh through change, or that it was changed into the whole man which consists of soul and body; but that the Word became man through uniting to itself the flesh, which was animated by the rational soul. . . . And that the natures which are united into this one true unity are different. And that there is one Christ and Son of both natures, not as though the differences of natures were removed through the union, but that through their ineffable unity the natures of divinity and humanity constitute for us the one Lord both Christ and Son. . . . It is not the case that first an ordinary man was born from the holy Virgin and that later the Word descended upon him; the Word united itself (with the humanity) from within the mother's womb and underwent a physical birth. . . . Thus (the holy Fathers) did not hesitate to call the holy Virgin the mother of God (**DS** 250, 251).

The **Council of Chalcedon** (451):

In imitation of the holy Fathers we confess that our Lord Jesus Christ is one and the same Son . . . , the same perfect in his divinity, perfect in his humanity: truly God and the same truly man of a rational soul and body; of one nature with the Father according to the divinity, and the same of one nature with us according to humanity. . . . (We profess) one and the same Christ, Son, Lord, Only-Begotten, in two natures, without confusion, without change, without division, and without separation. The

> difference in natures is not removed through the union, but the property of each nature is preserved and they coalesce in one person (**prosopon**) and one independence (**hupostasis**) (**DS** 301, 302).

The **Second Council of Constantinople** (680-681) to a great extent repeats the definition of Chalcedon (**DS** 421-438).

The **Third Council of Constantinople** (680-681) repeats again the definition of Chalcedon, but adds to it the pronouncement concerning the two wills and the two operations in Christ: We profess

> two natural wills in Him and two natural operations, without separation, without change, without division, and without confusion. . . . Not as though they would be contrary to one another, as the heretics maintain, but his human will follows and subjects itself to the divine and almighty will (**DS** 556; cf. 557).

However deserving of respect they may be, these formulae often arouse a sort of uneasiness, especially because only the arithmetical schema of the dogma is entrusted to us: one person in two natures. What fruit can this dogma bear for our profession of faith, for our personal relationship with Christ, and with our Christian existence? And yet this is precisely the connection in which this dogma must be fruitful, for it is in these words that the Church once and for all time has expressed her belief in her Savior and her salvation. These dogmatic formulae therefore must not be a dead letter, but a living and life-giving spirit.

In order to rediscover this spirit, history can be of some help to us. Then these sober words are seen to be overcome in the strenuous wrestling between the greatest and most saintly thinkers of Christianity, who deposited in a crystal-clear form in these formulae their insights of faith and their witness to Christ. And yet this history can easily disappoint us; for it is so full of misunderstanding, of hair-splitting and semantic squabbling, of conflicts between philosophical positions. All of these things increase our surprise at the importance which these saints and the Church itself attached to these formulae. And only in recent years, new facts have come to light which have even further confused this history. The task then will be to uncover the main lines of force which control the history of this dogma.

Grillmeier, and Kelly,[3] who has followed his lead, have depicted the conflict between the two conceptual schemas of Word-flesh and God-man as forming the main line of force. This conceptual conflict has indeed been of great significance; but the true source must lie deeper than in the opposition between Platonic and Aristotelian thought, namely in the very essence of what Jesus is for us. If with a

minimum of historical details, we succeed in making
it possible to see how this history was controlled by
the vision of the work of salvation, it may possibly
become apparent how the christological definitions
were actually the saving word concerning the Son
of God who is our Savior.

As Grillmeier correctly remarks in another study,
the greatness of patristic thought lies in the fact that
the highest dogmatic speculation of the Fathers was
nourished by the doctrine of salvation and the doctrine of salvation by dogmatic insight:[4] they are not
simply and not even primarily theological specialists,
but bishops and so pastors with a care for souls. But
few authors have attempted to approach the history
of Christology in the light of a vision of salvation.
This is what we wish to attempt in the following
pages. We feel that we can establish as dominating
motives in this historical development two fundamental visions of the mystery of the Redeemer: Jesus
is the man who is the Son of God; or Jesus is the
Word who reveals the Father in a human form.

I

THE FUNDAMENTAL VISIONS
TO 250

The apostolic preaching already employed a variety of ways to describe the mystery of Jesus' person and work. In the Synoptic and Pauline preaching, Jesus is primarily the Messiah and the Servant of God, the man who is raised up in the human race by God, who fulfills all justice and is obedient unto death, and who is established as Lord by God. The emphasis lies on the human life and activity of the Lord, not on his pre-existent or transcendent Sonship. In John, on the other hand, Jesus is the eternal Word and the eternal Son of the Father, who becomes flesh and appears in our midst and in whom the Father reveals himself. John's preference for the categories of light, truth, and knowledge is well known: "And eternal life is this, to know you, the only true God, and Jesus Christ whom you have sent" (John 17:3). Characteristic is the varying interpretation of Jesus' miracles: in the Synoptics they are deeds of power and authority ("The crowd . . . praised God for giving such power to men"—Matt. 9:8); in John they are graphic signs which present what God becomes for us in Jesus (the multiplication of the loaves: "I am the bread of life"—John 6:35). Characteristic also is the differing interpretation of cross and resurrection: on the one hand, obedience of man and the reward from God; on the other, rediscovery of the eternal glory which was veiled by the earthly flesh.

God, who works both in and through the Man as firstborn of humanity; the Word in which the Father speaks to us—these are the two main lines of force in the apostolic message about Jesus.

But although a certain opposition may seem to us to be present in these two considerations, this was not the case for Jewish thought, in which the one word **dabar** means "word" as well as "deed." For the Jew, the Word of God is a deed, and the deed of God is a revelation. God reveals himself as the Savior-God by saving; the preaching of the good news is the power of God (Rom. 1:15). To know God is to experience him and to accept him as the God who gives life.

As Christianity spread into the Hellenistic world, this original unity of speech and action became threatened. For Hellenistic intellectualism, speech was not action. Possibly the development of the christological dogma may be seen as the struggle against the disintegration of both main lines, as the attempt to recover the one completeness of the Jesus-image. It was, thus, the attempt to see in Jesus both the man who was raised up by God, who fulfilled that perfect obedience which constitutes our true humanity, and at the same time the Word through whom the Father speaks to us and reveals himself. Both motives are continually present in Catholic thought. But as long as these themes are not deepened and thought through to the point where they have an internal unity, theological reflection finds no peace. Thus as long as this internal unity has not yet been arrived at, tension and conflicts will crop up between those who regard the mystery of Christ from different points of view.

1. The Original Unity

In the first phase of christological reflection, the mysterious unity of God and man in Jesus was spontaneously and solidly affirmed. Ignatius of Antioch (d. **ca.** 110) can serve as an example:

> One is the physician,
>
> | of the flesh | and | of the spirit |
> | begotten | and | unbegotten |
> | in man | | God, |
> | in death | | the true life, |
> | as well from Mary | | as from God, |
> | first passible | | then impassible, |

Jesus Christ our Lord (**Eph.** 7, 2; Lightfoot, pp. 47f.).

Here Ignatius emphasizes the human aspect because he is fighting against the Docetic tendencies
which recognize in Jesus only an apparent body. But
the Son of God himself is the subject of this truly
human and truly physical life: "our God Jesus the
Christ was carried in Mary's womb, . . . was born
and was baptized" (**Eph.** 18, 2, Lightfoot, pp. 74f.).

His truly human life and activity is therefore an
address, a loud call from the Father: "The virginity
of Mary and her giving birth and also the death of
the Lord: three mysteries which are a loud scream
wrought in the silence of God" (**Eph.** 19, 1; Lightfoot,
pp. 76ff.).

The contrast between the mysteries, which in the
Hellenic world did indeed fall under the obligation
of silence, and the scream of God is certainly intended; and Ignatius chose a strong word to express
this: now that God himself makes salvation known,
the deafened world must awake with a start. For
through this Word, which becomes flesh and in
the flesh is obedient to the Father, the Father reveals
himself as a saving God: "There is one God, who
has made himself known through Jesus Christ his
Son, who is his Word that goes forth from the silence,
and that in all things is pleasing to God by whom
he was sent" (**Magn.** 8, 2; Lightfoot, pp. 125f.).

Jesus, the God in flesh, is "the mouth free from

lies, through which the Father has truly spoken"
(Rom. 8: 2; Lightfoot, p. 228).

Jesus, truly Son of God, both God and truly man,
who led a truly human life in perfect service and
obedience toward the Father, is at the same time
the mighty Word, which the Father speaks in the
world.

Traces of Ignatius' influence and imitations of the
passage cited above, in which he sets the divine and
human properties of the one incarnate Son of God
opposite one another, are found also in the following
centuries, in Melito of Sardis, Tertullian, Hippolytus.
But his greatest disciple is certainly Irenaeus of Lyon
(d. ca. 200).

Irenaeus' teaching about the incarnation and the
redemption at first perplexes the faithful of today
because the author incorporated therein elements
which we are not in the habit of mentioning in this
connection, and because the element of sacrifice,
which is most essential in our eyes, is almost completely absent from the writing of Irenaeus. But upon
further study, Irenaeus' teaching appears to be the
most harmonious and richest of the entire ancient
period. In his polemic against the Gnostic errors,
he re-emphasizes continually the theme of unity: the
unity of the Creator-God and the heavenly Father,
the unity of the Old and the New Covenants, the

unity of the body and the soul in man, the ultimate
unity of this whole man with the Father, which is
the principle of man's creation and redemption. And
the keystone of comprehensive unity is the one Jesus
Christ:

> The Word, who was in the beginning with
> God, and through whom all things were
> created, and who at all times has helped the
> human race, that Word has at the end of time
> . . . united himself with his creation and be-
> come a mortal man. . . . And by becoming man,
> he restored anew the lengthy series of men in
> himself and brought them under one head
> (**recapitulavit**), and in short has given us salva-
> tion. Thus we regain in Christ Jesus what we
> had lost in Adam, namely existence according
> to God's image and likeness (**Adv. Haereses
> III. 18, 1**).

In this synthesis many thoughts are interconnected.
From eternity the Son glorified his Father (IV. 14, 1)
and in the creation of the world and of man working
as the hand of the Father, he brought his plan to
actualization (IV. 20, 1). But because of his foolish
disobedience man lost his likeness to God, and thus
brought himself eternal death. For as "one who sees
God, is in God, and shares in his splendor and thus
participates in life" (IV. 20, 5), so is "separation from
God death and separation from the light darkness"
(V. 27, 2).

But despite his fall "Adam did not escape from the hand of God" (V. 1, 3). The Word continued to remain busy with man and allowed sin to ripen so that man could experience his weakness to the full extreme, and thus could stand open for God's grace (V. 3, 1). Then finally the eternal Son of God became man, actually a child of our race and of our flesh and blood (V. 14, 2-3), but born of a virgin, because in salvation the initiative lay completely with God (III. 21, 6-7).

In various ways, which though differing still have an internal bond between them, Irenaeus describes how the incarnate Son of God saves us. Irenaeus does this in the first place by using the concept of "recapitulation," which literally means "to bring under the head again," "collection," "restoration," but which also includes the proposition that the incarnate Son, as the second Adam, re-enacts in reverse direction the process of Adam's fall and thus undoes it: his life is like a positive of the negative of Adam's sin:

> As through the disobedience of one man sin entered and through sin death has established her dominion, so through the obedience of one man obedience was again introduced and has borne the fruit of life for men. . . . And as the first Adam was formed out of unworked and still virgin soil, . . . so was the Word born from Mary, who was still a virgin . . . (III. 21, 10).

In this process the obedience of the Virgin Mary is the counterpart of the disobedience of Eve (III. 22, 4; V. 19, 1), and the tree of the cross the counterpart of the tree from which Adam ate (V. 17, 3; **Epideixis** 34). Therefore the Word-become-man passes through every period and every phase of human life, presenting himself to all as an example and saving all (II. 22, 4). Finally in obedience he undergoes death, which resulted from Adam's disobedience:

> Because it was impossible for man, who once through disobedience was conquered and fell, to renew himself and to regain the palm of victory; and because it was further impossible for one who had fallen under sin to attain salvation; therefore the Son who is the Word of God, by becoming man and by descending to death has accomplished both of these things (III. 17, 2).

The interpretation of Jesus' death as a sacrifice appears only rarely in the works of Irenaeus (IV. 5, 4; 8, 2); this death is, rather, for Irenaeus the consequence of Adam's disobedience which is brought into obedience by the incarnate Son (III. 22, 4).

Another theme which Irenaeus uses could be called that of the "exchange" theory. This will become of the greatest dogmatic importance:

> The Word of God therefore has become man and God's Son the son of man, in order

that, by embracing the Word and receiving adoptive childhood, man could become son of God. . . . For how could we become participants in imperishableness and immortality (these words signify in Irenaeus what later writers will call "deification") if the imperishable and the immortal did not first become what we are (III. 19, 1)?

The Word of God, our Lord Jesus Christ, because of his boundless love became what we are in order to make us what he is (V. **Praef.**).

In himself he brought about the unity between the Father and the humanity of Adam, and so gave us the possibility of becoming children of God, "uniting man with God" (IV. 20, 4). The Holy Spirit, whom he received in fullness in his humanity as a gift of the Father, he pours out on those who are his. The Spirit makes us acceptable to the Father and leads us to him (III. 17, 1-2).

Between the recapitulation theory and the exchange theory there is a connection. The Word, who is our Creator, and thus contains within himself the idea of true humanity, himself becomes man, even unto the extreme of death. Through this he realizes in himself the true and absolute humanity: obedience and filial dependence toward the Father. And because of this he stands henceforth as the new Adam in the heart of mankind, giving us a share in his filial relationship with the Father.

We receive this sharing through faith, baptism, and the Eucharist, and by following Jesus' law and example. Through faith we recognize him, and in him the Father:

> For we could not be instructed in the things of God, if our teacher, the Word, had not become man. For no one else could tell us things of the Father, other than his own Word. . . . And we, from our side, could not otherwise be instructed than by seeing our teacher and by hearing his voice with our ears (V. 1, 1).

For the sake of the physical man, God speaks in the flesh. But "in the flesh of our Lord, the light of the Father meets us and from that flesh shines out over us; thus man arrives at imperishableness because he is irradiated by the light of the Father" (IV. 20, 2).

Besides our fleshly weakness there is yet another reason for this veiling of the divine brilliance: it reveals the Father to us, and still causes us to understand that he dwells in unapproachable light; it gives us the certainty of God's nearness, but calls us still to unfathomed depths of intimacy (IV. 20, 7). Precisely because the Son becomes man, Christian existence remains dynamically drawn toward a homecoming and reunion with the Father.

That Jesus is our lawgiver and example follows automatically from the preceding. As the original Word of God who stands at the origin of mankind, he realizes in his own humanity the proper divine idea of man. We must "follow the Word of God" (IV. 16, 5; 28, 2). For "to follow the Savior is to share in salvation" (IV. 14, 1). Thus God is "glorified in his creature in that he makes it similar in form to and docile toward his Son-Servant" (V. 6, 1).[5] Thus "man becomes dear to the Father through likeness with the Son" (V. 15, 2). Thus we have "community with him by imitating his deeds and carrying out his words" (V. 1, 1), who "graciously pours himself out over us in order to gather us to the bosom of the Father" (V. 2, 1). Thus "the Son leads us to the Father" and the veil will be removed and we will "see God and through this vision live" (IV. 20, 5-6).

In this great synthesis of creation, salvation history, incarnation, and redemption, the great moments of the mystery of Christ are harmoniously blended together. The kernel of Irenaeus' vision is that actually "one and the same" (III. 16, 7-8; 17, 4) Word of Creation is both man and flesh and blood and soul: precisely in this way indeed humanity is realized in him in an absolute completeness, and he can become for all a source of life and an example, thus a new Adam. Here it is essential that the subject of

the incarnation is the Word and the Son in whom
the Father expresses himself and who lives as a son
on earth. It is also necessary that he become fully
man with soul and flesh and blood, that he be one of
our race unto our death. For the sin of Adam is
conquered because one of his children in filial
obedience and subjection expiates the consequences
of Adam's rebellion. Finally it becomes quite clear
here that the incarnation and the human life of Jesus
is a self-revelation of the Father who manifests himself in him as the Creator and Savior and Lifegiver,
and who thus prepares man for the unveiled vision
of the Father.

Unfortunately Irenaeus did not establish a school.
One does hear in later writers the echo of various
of Irenaeus' descriptions and even of his phrasing.
But only his teaching that Jesus is not "one and
another" becomes universal common property. The
unity of the subject, which after all was an evident
datum of Scripture, is rarely disputed any more within the Church before Nestorius. Recollections of
Irenaeus' teaching about the recapitulation or the
exchange or the parallelism between the first and the
second Adam can be found in quantity. But these
elements are no longer bound together in one great
synthetic vision. Instead each element goes its separate way and only after centuries will there be a

rediscovery of something of the brilliance which sweeps through Irenaeus' work. In the course of their long meanderings these separate elements will be further deepened and developed, but for the time they lose more than a little of their original richness.

The theology of the West will concentrate its attention, on the one hand, on the human actions of Jesus and especially on his crucifixion and sacrifice and, on the other hand, on the static analysis of the union between the divine person (they rarely ask why precisely the Son has become man) and the man in Jesus. Greek theology, on the other hand, will turn its eye in particular on the person of the Word and his function in revelation. When this threatens to lead to a flight from the human reality of Jesus, the Greek world will go in two separate directions: the one, in an excessive reaction, will move toward an overemphasis of the human independence of Jesus' existence and action; the other will recover something of Irenaeus' insight that the fundamental principle of our salvation is the ontological union of the Word with mankind, but it will still have difficulty in integrating into its vision the significance of Jesus' human activity.

2. Christology in the West

a. Hippolytus of Rome (d. ca. 235)

Hippolytus is the one who stands closest to

Irenaeus, especially in the former's dramatic vision of the event of the incarnation:

> The Word leaped down from heaven into the womb of the Virgin, he leaped from his mother's womb onto the wood, he leaped from the wood into the netherworld, he leaped upwards again to the earth . . . and leaped again from earth to heaven. Thus he goes to sit in power at the right hand of the Father (**In Cant. 2, 8**).[6]

The Jesus who was born, died, and rose is thus truly the eternal Word of the Father, "God become man": from the Father according to the "heavenly," from Mary and from the old Adam according to the "earthly." For our sake he became like ourselves, formed from the old stuff of Adam, truly man, just as he showed by experiencing every human need.

Hippolytus has scarcely any technical terminology to express the unity of the Word with humanity, but in many passages he places the personal pronoun "he" at the beginning with great emphasis as the bearer of the divine as well as of the human nature; the Word-became-man is one single subject. This one Jesus

> had both in himself, as well the substance (**ousia**) of God as that of man, as the apostle also says: "mediator of God and man, the man Jesus Christ." But someone is a mediator not

of one man, but of two. Therefore Christ, who
was the mediator of God and of men, had to
get a pledge (**arrabôn**) from both, in order to
appear as mediator of two persons" (**Fragm. in
Balaam,** ed. Achelis, **GCS** I, 2, p. 82).[7]

The reason for this incarnation is our salvation,
which Hippolytus describes in many ways: re-creation
of Adam, new birth through the Holy Spirit, revelation of the Father, life through the death on the
cross, resurrection in the Risen One, imperishableness,
deification. Except for the last word, these are all
terms from Irenaeus. But there is a change in emphasis. The human actions of Jesus now have the
function of establishing the reality of his human
nature and of giving us an example of genuine humanity (**Elenchos** X. 33/15-17; a copy of Irenaeus, **Adv.
Haereses** II. 22/4): example, which was only second-
ary in Irenaeus, here becomes the most important
factor. There is no trace of the objective saving
power of Jesus' life which makes our life holy because
the Son has lived it in a holy manner. At the same
time the insight that a life with the Son leads to the
Father disappears: here it is docility toward God
through which we are deified:

> God has made you man, but if you more-
> over desire to become God, then be obedient
> to your Maker.

> If you observe his commandments and

through your goodness imitate him who is good, . . . he will make you God, to his glory (**Elench.** X. 33/7; 34/5).

While the saving power of the life of Jesus recedes into the background, that of the cross comes to the fore. Jesus, who indeed "is the will of the Father," is "the perfect king and priest, the only one who has fulfilled the will of the Father." And in addition to being the priest, he is also the true Paschal Lamb: he has "in himself offered man to the Father"; "he himself offered himself up to the Father." Through this sacrifice, through the cross, resurrection and ascension, he has in himself completed salvation, achieving the union of human flesh and divine nature, which he had begun in the womb of the Virgin:

The spiritual Word of God has taken on flesh from the holy Virgin, as the bridegroom does his clothing. And he has set it off from himself in his suffering on the cross, in order to save lost man, by uniting our mortal flesh with his own Power (=divinity). . . . His suffering on the cross is like the loom of the Lord, the power of the Holy Spirit in him like the warp, the grace of Christ's love like the thread, which binds together and unites both into one, the Word like the weaver's needle, the patriarchs and prophets, who weave the long and perfect cloth of Christ, like the laborers (**De Antichristo,** 4th ed., Bonwetsch-Achelis, **GCS** I. 2, pp. 6f.).

b. Tertullian (d. after 220)

Tertullian was also a disciple of Irenaeus, but his interest was far more directed to the manner of the incarnation than toward its saving significance. In the beginning of his Christian career he had already formulated the Christian teaching as follows for his pagan readers:

> This ray of God (the relationship between the Father and the Word was compared to that between the sun and a ray of sunlight), as has been previously stated, came down into a virgin, and in her womb was formed into flesh (**caro figuratus**). He was born as a man who is mixed with God (**homo Deo mixtus;** in the early centuries the term "to mix" was a favorite one to express the intimacy of the union). The flesh, formed through the Spirit, is fed, grows up, begins to speak, teaches, performs miracles, and is Christ (**Apologet.** 21/14).

Later in his career Tertullian twice treats at length of Christ. Against the heretics, who did not want to recognize in Jesus a real man of flesh and blood, Tertullian argues that Jesus has "two substances," the divine and the human (**De Carne Christi** 18/6f; cf. 1/2). But is it not apparent from his virginal birth that Christ is not a real man? "No," responds Tertullian: that he was born from a mother means that he truly is a man of our race; that his mother was a virgin signifies that he is also the Son of God in addition to being the son of man (**De Carne Christi** 14/5).

> As before his birth from the virgin he had God as Father without a human mother, so when he was born from the virgin he could have a human being as mother without having a human father (**De Carne Christi** 18/2).

Tertullian's opponents pose still another problem: God cannot become man because by becoming what he was not he would cease to be what he was. The answer states that this principle indeed is valid for created things, but that God is completely different so that "God can change into all things and still remain as he is" (**De Carne Christi** 3/4-6).

Apart from the word "change," which he himself will later discard, this is a deeply significant thought. Or is it—with Tertullian one can never be certain— no more than a cleverly worded formula? Whichever it may be, Tertullian was apparently throughout his life intensely concerned with the manner in which the incarnation took place.

As a result of these reflections, he developed formulae toward the end of his career which appeared to be nearly definitive. His book **Against Praxeas** is devoted to the distinction and the union of Father, Son, and Holy Spirit, and thus also treats of the incar-

nation. As the Son of God is not "an other" than
the man Jesus (**Adv. Prax.** 27/2; cf. **De Carne Christi**
24/3), but has become man, does this "becoming"
then mean that the Son is changed into flesh? Tertullian responds in the negative, for through change
the Son would have ceased to be what he was before
and Jesus would

> have only one substance (**substantia**), which
> comes from two, from spirit (=divinity) and
> flesh; then he would thus be a hybrid . . ., that
> is, neither spirit nor flesh, because the one is
> changed by the other, and so a third substance
> would come into being. Then Jesus would not
> be God, for by becoming flesh he would have
> ceased to be the Word; nor would he be flesh
> and man, for actually he would not be flesh
> because he is the Word (27/6-9).

A change and mixture of this sort is contrary to
Scripture, which names him God as well as man,

> in every aspect Son of God and Son of Man,
> God and man according to both substances,
> each of which is distinguished through its
> properties: for the Word is not something other
> than God, nor the flesh something other than
> man. . . . We find a twofold manner of being,
> not confused but united in one person (**dupli-
> cem statum, non confusum sed coniunctum in
> una persona**) Jesus, God and Man. . . . And
> that which is proper to each of the two sub-

stances is preserved intact (**salva est utriusque proprietas substantiae**), in such a way that the spirit (=divinity) in him has done what is proper to it, namely miraculous works and signs, and the flesh has also undergone what is proper to it, being hungry, thirsty, weeping, being oppressed unto death, and finally dying (27/11).

In these formulations, which via Leo the Great will press into the definition of Chalcedon, it is emphatically stated that Jesus, who is truly God and truly man, is nonetheless a single subject: not "one and another" but "one person." It is also clear that this union does not signify a violation either of the divinity or of the humanity in their respective properties. Jesus, the Son of God and God, is truly man, and undergoes everything that is human up to and including death. One can thus say that "God allows himself to be born" from Mary (**De Patientia** 3/2) and that "the Son of God has died" (**Adv. Prax.** 29/1): the one subject, that is the Son of God, experiences what is human. "But it is clear to what extent the apostle calls him dead, namely as flesh and man and son of man, not as Spirit and Word and Son of God" (**Adv. Prax.** 29/2).

In contrast to this penetrating analysis of the manner of the incarnation, Tertullian's explanations concerning the reason for the incarnation make a very

poor impression. He repeats one of the great recapitulation texts of Irenaeus (**De Carne Christi**
17/2-6). He is also aware that the incarnate Son of
God is the firstborn of regenerated and glorified
mankind:

> There Jesus sits at the right hand of the Father,
> man, although God, the last Adam, although
> the first Word, flesh and blood, although more
> pure than our own. . . . He is named the media-
> tor of God and men, because of the pledge
> that is entrusted to him from both sides. And
> he also preserves in himself the pledge of the
> flesh, as earnest-money on the principal. For
> as he has left us the earnest-money of the
> Spirit, so he has accepted from us the earnest-
> money of the flesh and brought it into heaven
> as earnest-money on the principal which at one
> time, through the resurrection, will enter there.
> You can be safe, flesh and blood: in Christ you
> have gained possession of heaven and the king-
> dom of God (**De Resurr. Mort.** 51/1-3; cf. **Adv.
> Marc.** III 9/4).

But in this saving work of the Lord, the actual
emphasis nonetheless rests not upon the fact that
the Son has accepted human existence up to and
including death but, rather, upon the cross as such.
Through his blood he has ransomed; because the
Innocent has endured what was due to us sinners,
he has broken our chains. Tertullian is thus able to

present as the only grounds for the incarnation the
reason that Christ had to die: "Christ, who was sent
in order to die, also necessarily had to be born in
order to be able to die: for only that which has been
born is accustomed to die. . . . His intended death
is the cause of his birth" (**De Carne Christi** 6/6).

And yet one does Tertullian an injustice to say
"that for him the meaning of Redemption is narrowed
down to remission of sins"[8] or that his conception of
the cross calls up the image of "the wrathful God
who had to be appeased."[9] Nor does Tertullian
consider the cross apart from the resurrection, or the
forgiveness of sins apart from rebirth to eternal life.
Even with regard to the passage just quoted about
death as the motive for Jesus' birth, there was a
more complete formulation which immediately preceded it: Christ came on earth "to experience death,
and to be raised up from out of death" (**De Carne
Christi** 6/5).

It is not only the cross, but also the resurrection
which is the principle of Christian grace; so Christian
baptism could not be given before Easter,

> because the glorification of the Lord was not
> yet completed and because the water was not
> yet filled with power through his suffering
> and resurrection: indeed our death cannot be
> undone unless by the suffering of the Lord,

nor can our life be renewed without his resurrection (**De Bapt.** 11/4; cf. **Adv. Marc.** III
8/5-7).

But the fact is that the mystery of death and resurrection receives such a strong emphasis that the incarnation is seen almost exclusively in function thereof
(see however **De Carne Christi** 16/4). In Tertullian
there is no mention of a sanctification of human life
due to the fact that the Son of God has lived as man.
Therefore all that the Lord has done as man has
scarcely any meaning for salvation; only what he has
suffered has salvific significance. Likewise Tertullian
has little eye for the mysterious, nearly organic bond
which the incarnation effected between the Son of
God and the family of man. It is precisely when he
argues that Jesus was truly born of Mary that there
is such a remarkable absence of any reference to the
Son taking on **our** flesh: he had to be born in order
truly to be a man and thus to be able to die and to
rise, but not in order to be incorporated into the
family of Adam through ties of blood. Naturally
Tertullian knows that Jesus is our high priest and
our representative, but he does not search for a
deeper union in being. Herein lurks the danger that
Jesus is a representative only in a juridical and
arbitrary manner. Actually Tertullian gives no answer
to the essential question about the reason for the
incarnation: Why did our Savior have to taste our

death? Why was it necessary for our Savior to be
God, and God the Son in particular? Tertullian's
only answer states that in order to take away our
sins our Savior had to be without sin. But this answer
is certainly quite poor. And this demand for sinlessness is the only connection which Tertullian was
able to establish between the incarnation and the
redemption.

Tertullian's teaching about the incarnation offers
a penetrating analysis and marvelous statement of
the formal, static aspect of the incarnation. In contrast to this, his explanation of the relationship between incarnation and redemption is very poor; thus
his reflection on the existential ground of the mystery
of the Son-become-man is very weak. Because of
this, Tertullian's teaching is a dangerous heritage
through which his heirs can be led continually to
refine the analysis of the "how" of the incarnation but
to neglect its meaning for salvation. They will thus
be led to sever the theological reflection on the
mystery of Jesus from the womb of faith from which
it draws its life. In the full bloom of the patristic
period this danger was easily avoided. Even if the
leading Christian thinkers of the period do make
grateful use of Tertullian's rational framework, they
are such good pastors of souls and such great saints
that they do not allow themselves to be forced into

the narrow passageway of his purely formal and
static description of the incarnation. But Scholasticism
will often become the prisoner of Tertullian's heritage, whenever it fails to allow itself to be nourished
from other sources (as Thomas did in drawing upon
Cyril of Alexandria).

c. Cyprian (d. 258)

Though an enthusiastic admirer and normally
faithful imitator of Tertullian, Cyprian still displays
a very significant independence precisely in his teaching about the redemption. His short clarifications
are more dynamic and personal. In the incarnation
and the passion "Christ bore us and all our sins"
(**Ep.** 63, 13/.). By "offering himself up to the Father
as the High Priest of God the Father" (**Ep.** 63, 4/4)
he has conquered sin and death. We share in this
victory, through the fact that we put him on and
follow in his footsteps: thus the goal of Jesus' sacrifice is realized in us according to this law of exchange
which we saw in Irenaeus: "The Son of God became
man in order to make us sons of God" (**Ep.** 58, 6/3).

Cyprian does not speak of a rather abstract deification, but of a participation in the Sonship of the
Son, which is thus crowned by a personal relationship
to the Father. Cyprian sees Jesus' saving deeds as
laden with meaning. Thus Jesus' ascension had the
significance of placing "man, whom he loved and took

on and saved from death, victoriously by the Father"
(**Quod idola** 14).[10] This "man" is Jesus' own humanity,
but it is also all of us, whom Jesus did indeed bear.

The minor variations which Cyprian introduced
when imitating passages of Tertullian (and possibly
of Hippolytus) are of some significance:

> The Word and the Son of God . . . is God's
> power, his Logos, his Wisdom and his Glory.
> The Word descends into the virgin; the Holy
> Spirit takes on flesh; God unites himself with
> man. He is our God, he is Christ, who as
> mediator of both, has taken on man in order
> to lead him to the Father. What man is,
> Christ desired to be, in order that man could
> be what Christ is (**Quod idola** 11).

This goal is not referred to as a deification, but as
being led to the Father, an approaching him with and
in his Son Christ. Cyprian also shows that a richer
and warmer vision of Christ's work and person was
alive in the Latin Church than Tertullian's writings
would have led one to suspect.

3. The Word-Christology of Alexandria

Already in the Apostolic Fathers, the reader is
confronted with the heavy emphasis which falls upon
Jesus' function as teacher and even as moralist. It
almost seems as if the Fathers are unaware of his
job as Redeemer. But this conclusion would be

justifiable only if we could apply our contemporary criteria to their time. For them the moral law was a large portion of redemption. From Paul of Augustine, a vital role was played by the concept that man's slavery under sin consisted in large part in his blindness: an ignorance which is not exculpating but which itself is an element of guilt (Rom. 1: 21). A scholar well versed in early Christian thought writes: "Forgiveness signifies not merely the cancelling of penalty, but the cure of that ignorance, which is the cause and strength of sin."[11] In this world, knowledge of good and evil could serve as redemption.

What in the Apostolic Fathers was a one-sided look at the totality of the redemption became, in the quasi-Christian sects of Gnosticism, a highly developed system. For the various Gnostic schools, salvation and knowledge are identical. For them, man is a being of divine nature, which is alienated from itself through ignorance and association with the body. Return to oneself through self-knowledge, then, is rediscovery of the divine, is eternal life and salvation. The saving

> gnosis is the knowledge of who we are and what we are becoming, of where we come from and where we are going, of that to which we are redeemed, how it stands with our birth and our rebirth (quoted in Clement of Alexandria, Exc. ex Theod. 78/2).

In these Gnostic systems the only task of the
Savior will be to instruct the ignorant man concerning
his proper nature and about the divine reality of
which he is a part. Here the Redeemer does not have
to be man; in fact he may not be a man of flesh and
blood: he is a messenger from the divine world, who
has nothing to do with the prison of the body which
holds us captive in ignorance. At most, in order to
speak to us, he has taken on an apparent body.
(Docetism, from the Greek **docein** = "to appear," "to
seem.")

Immediately a strong resistance arose within the
Church against this denial of the human and physical
reality of the Lord. John the evangelist seems already
to have directed himself against this; and the Christology of Ignatius, Irenaeus, and Tertullian is quite
definitely directed against this falsification of the
evangelical image of the Lord.

And yet the appeal of such conceptions seems to
have been unusually strong. Knowledge and ignorance played such a great role in the Hellenic world
that Catholic thinkers also presented redemption
primarily as enlightenment and knowledge. They
described redemption not as a knowledge about a
pantheistically considered substance of man, or about
a strange unnamable godhead, but as knowledge
about the God who has created us and our world

and who wills to be our Father. They go on to describe the work of Jesus primarily as a revelation of the Father and speak of his Person as the Word through which the Father speaks to us.

A characteristic example is the manner in which Justin Martyr (d. **ca.** 165) clarifies the distinction between the Old and the New Covenants. He knows well enough that Jesus was born from Mary and has redeemed us through his cross. But he characterizes the period before the coming of Jesus as the time in which the Word revealed himself only partially to the Jews through the prophets and to the pagans through their inborn reason (the Greek term **Logos**= "Word"; it also means "reason"), while now He has come himself and thus "has appeared fully," "become body and reason and soul for us," in order that even the unlettered and the working class could know him (**Apol.** II. 10; 13). This fullness of revelation is the characteristic property of the New Dispensation: revelation is the heart of the work of salvation. Due to the fact that it was systematically worked out in the school of Alexandria, this vision will become one of the determining factors of the later christological development.

a. Clement of Alexandria (d. **ca.** 220)

Clement's thought is characterized less by a systematic approach than it is by associative relation-

ships. He thus makes no systematic effort to fit his
faith in Christ into the framework of a Word-theology.
But there is still an unmistakable tendency in this
direction. And this is even more remarkable in light
of the fact that he sometimes can speak of the
incarnation, the cross, and the eucharistic body and
blood of Christ in lyric ecstasy. Clement is also
familiar with the exchange theory of Irenaeus. But
this is continually placed within the framework of
the theme that Jesus teaches us to live in accordance
with the Logos, which he himself is, and thus makes
us, through an imitation of and a process of becoming
like God, suitable for the ultimate vision of the
Father (**Paedag.** I. 12, 98/3; 100/3; III. 1, 1/5).

Clement is aware that the Mediator, "God in a
man, and the Man God," has freed the flesh from the
slavery of death because he "suffered with" the flesh
(**Paedag.** III. 1, 2/1-3); through his pains he has given
us rebirth and wrapped us in the bandages of his
blood (**Paedag.** I. 6, 42/2; 29/4); he has entrusted
himself to the Church, the mother, as food and drink
for her children (**ibid.**). But the dominating motif in
these passages is likewise that the Logos nourishes
us with his teaching and, as our disciplinarian, teaches
us: "He crucified death unto life, . . . changed muta-
bility into immutability, and earth into heaven, . . .
and he gave us the divine and inalienable heritage

of the Father by deifying man through his heavenly
teaching" (**Protrept.** 11, 114/4).

Another very characteristic passage is one in which
the love of the Father is presented as the principle
of the incarnation:

> God is love, and because of this love he
> allowed himself to be revealed. . . . And one
> great sign of this is (the Son), whom he bore
> from out himself: and he who is born as the
> fruit of love, who is himself love. It is for
> this reason that he also came down, it is for
> this reason that he took on a man, it is for
> this reason that he voluntarily suffered what
> is human: namely in order to adapt himself to
> the stature of our weakness, and thus, on the
> other hand, to adapt us to his Power (=divinity).
> And then when he was at the point of emptying
> himself and giving himself as a ransom, he left
> us a new last will and testament: "My love I
> give to you,"

which Clement understands to be the commandment
of love (**Quis dives** 37/1-4).

The incarnation and the cross as self-revelation of
the love of the Father, who has begotten his eternal
Son as fruit and image of his love, and who now
abandons his Son to the horror of our mortality—this
is a wonderful and deeply Christian vision. But even
here, this image ends in a moral lesson: imitate this

divine love. It is no wonder, therefore, that no other
motive is elsewhere given for the incarnation than
that of our education ("education" is of course not
to be understood in an academic sense): "The Word
of God became man so that you also could learn
from a man how man becomes God" (**Protrept.** 1, 8/4).

In this passage also, the manner in which reference
is made to the exchange theory of Irenaeus is characteristic. For Clement, in spite of several additions
(e.g., **Paedag.** I. 5, 18/4), there is no ontological participation in the incarnate Son. This is a palpable
appearance of the love of the Father, and an example
for us who as children strive after a likeness with
the Father.

But in this way it becomes quite difficult to
attribute their full meaning to the incarnation, the
cross, and the resurrection. Could the Word not teach
us without becoming man? Is the only reason for
his incarnation the fact that he adapts himself to our
fleshly state, in which we can hear the Word in no
other way than in the form of flesh? In Clement
there is a danger of a flight from the earthly existence
and the earthly deeds of the Lord, which are
spiritualized into images of the divine reality. And
accompanying this, even as Clement expressly argues
against the Gnostics who reduce the human into an
apparent form, there is the threat of a flight from

Jesus' humanity which becomes only a mouthpiece and a means of revelation (**Stromat.** III. 17, 102/3).

b. Origen (d. ca. 254)

In this genial disciple of Clement there is an even stronger threat of flight from the human reality of Jesus. And yet Origen manages to avoid this danger with the aid of a consistently developed Word-Christology. Before we sketch this theology, we should first mention something about some other aspects of his vision of Christ.

Because Jesus is everything for us, he cannot be described in any one concept: he is for us God, Wisdom, Word, Life; but he is also Redeemer, Physician, Firstborn of the dead. This last series of titles became proper to him only because man had sinned (**Comm. Jo.** I. 20).[12]

> If there were no sin it would not be necessary that the Son of God became a lamb; and that he be sacrificed in the flesh, but he would then have remained what he was in the beginning, God's Word. But because sin has entered into the world and because sin necessarily demanded propitiation, and because propitiation came about only through a victim, it was therefore necessary to find a victim for sin. (The old sacrifices were an expression of this search for reconciliation, but now they have ceased being of service), now the Lamb

has come, who can take away the sins of the
whole world . . . and who alone is sufficient
for the salvation of the whole world (**Hom.
Num.** 24, 1).

Having become man, he could take away sin, because he himself is without sin (**Comm. Jo. XXVIII.**
18), because he is the powerful one who can bind and
banish the enemy (**Hom. Levit.** 9, 5), because at one
and the same time, as man he is the Lamb and as
Son of God he is "the great high priest" (**Comm. Jo.
VI.** 53, 274). Because he is the only high priest,
every worthy sacrifice must "be offered up by Jesus
Christ to almighty God, because according to his
divinity he has access to the Father" (**Gesprek met
Heracl.** 4).

Origen dedicated rich pages to the discussion of
the sacrifice of Christ. But the signficance of this
sacrifice consisted in the atonement of sin. Positively
stated, this goal is the redemption of mankind; and
this redemption consisted in the union with God, with
the Father. This union can likewise be described in
a variety of ways. In the ascension of Jesus, Origen
sees the gesture by which the Son consecrates in
himself the pledge of our flesh to the Father (**Hom.
Levit.** 9, 5). And the fundamental act of this salvation
consisted in the incarnation itself, thus in the ontological union with the Son. Here Origen has given

form to an idea of Irenaeus, which will appear to be of great importance nearly a century later: Because the Lord wanted to give salvation to the whole man, to the body, soul and spirit, he has thus likewise taken on all these components of the human substance because "the whole man would not be saved if he had not taken on the whole man" (**Gesprek met Heracl.** 7).

But Origen's true preference is for another description. Our salvation consists in union with God the Father, through which union we know the Father, and in which we become deified. And the way to the Father is the incarnate Son:

> Then (in heaven) there will be only one occupation for those who have come to God through the Word which is with God, namely to behold God (**katanoein**), so that thus everyone, transformed through knowledge of the Father, precisely becomes a son, as now only the Son knows the Father. . . . (Now we do not yet know the Father), but only when we all will be one as the Father and the Son are one (**Comm. Jo.** I. 16, 92-93).

To know the Father through and with and in the Son, this is salvation. Of course "knowledge" here (as is also the case in Clement) means much more than merely "to know": an all-inclusive union of person with person, which includes understanding,

likeness, love, and which also signifies deification
for men: man "becomes deified in what he beholds"
(**Comm. Jo.** XXXII. 27, 338). "Knowledge for Origen
is 'to be similar, to unite oneself.' "[13]

From this point the vision of Origen is grand and
simple. From the divine Father proceeds the Son,
who is the perfect Image of the Father and who is
united in divine intimacy with the Father, because he
"beholds without interruption the depth of the Father"
(**Comm. Jo.** II. 2, 18). This Son becomes man, that
is to say, he takes on a human soul and by means of
this soul also a true human body. In this union the
relationship of image to original Image repeats itself:
the soul of Jesus is completely sinless and is therefore
a pure image of the eternal Image of the Father;
Jesus' soul thus reveals without interruption that
Image to which it lovingly clings with all its being.
And the body of Jesus in its turn is the expression
and the mirror of his soul.[14] The goal of this incarnation is the salvation of fallen man: the eternal Image
of the Father appears in the image of the Image and
in the flesh, in order that we may know in physical,
human form the Son and in him the Father:

> He who came down among men was in
> the form of God. But because of his love of
> men he emptied himself in order that men
> could accept him. . . . (This does not indicate

any change in the Word). But the Word
descends to the level of man, who is incapable
of seeing the radiant glory of the divinity, and
becomes flesh so to speak, so that it may be
spoken in physical terms. But one who receives
him in this form is step by step raised on high
by the Word and can finally behold his absolute form (C. Celsum IV. 15).

Our salvation therefore consists in our climbing
up to the Father by means of the steps of Jesus'
bodiliness, of his interior and divine Sonship. Our
Redeemer is thus all the steps himself (Comm. Jo.
XIX. 6, 38-39); he continually adapts himself to the
capacities of those who are his: for some, milk; for
others, a healing herb; for the perfect, solid food
(C. Celsum IV. 18).

Jesus' bodiliness is thus the point at which the
Word unites himself with the family of men, the
bridal chamber where the Church receives a share
in the Word, through whom she comes to the Father
(In Cant. III, Baehrens, GCS 33, p. 176); or his physical form is likewise the window through which the
Bridegroom lets his Bride see his face. Jesus' humanity is the example which men must imitate and with
which they must unite themselves in order to attain
oneness with the Word and with the Father:

With him the divine and the human natures
began to become interwoven, in order that the

human might be deified through community
with the divine, not in Jesus alone, but in
everyone who, after having believed, received
the life which he has taught, and which leads
on high to community with God and friendship with him (**C. Celsum** III. 28).

In this way also the ideal of creation is realized
in us, where man exists according to the image and
likeness of God.

There are surprising elements in this synthesis,
which will be seen to be important for the future, at
the same time both fruitful and dangerous. Origen's
synthesis forms the starting point of the later christological debates. All the errors as well as all the great
orthodox teachers will claim to find support in him.
Therefore we must pause here for a little longer.

Incarnation and redemption are here logically
thought out in the categories of image, revelation,
and vision. For a proper understanding of Origen,
one must also consider that for him an intimate bond
exists between image and vision. For in Origen's
thought "being-an-image" is a dynamic reality, and
a vision is a total dedication to the one beheld, a
loving and lucid spiritual assimilation. Perfectly
being-an-image is perfect vision: for where there is a
spiritual Being-an-image, it is a truly spiritual, thus
conscious and free, self-possessing and self-realizing

likeness with the original Image, thus a being-like-in-form which essentially includes a loving making-like-in-form.

Thus the Son is one with the Father, not in a purely statically considered oneness-in-nature, but in a dialogue between the Father, who totally expresses himself in his Word, and the Son, who assents to his own proper essence in a divinely perfect way, thus says Yes to his own proper Sonship and to the Father. Later followers of Origen will conceive of this unity of the Son with his Father as a purely moral union, and deny the oneness in nature. Origen himself does not deny the oneness in nature, on the contrary; but the nature is divine, intellectual, free: oneness-in-nature is thus a conscious and free (not a contingently, but a divinely, free) unity.[15]

In an analogous manner the union of the human soul with the Word is not a purely static unity. It is a spiritual union and therefore a unity which is consciously and lovingly assented to. Jesus' soul is totally filled with the divine person of the Son in knowing, loving, and acting. So intimate is this unity that the Son dwells in this humanity "substantially" and totally, in contrast to the saints who only receive a participation of the Son:

> The soul is like iron in the fire. . . . (in the fire, iron itself, with retention of its own

matter, becomes fire), always in the Word, always in Wisdom, always in God. . . . All the saints have received something of the warmth of God's Word, but in this soul the divine fire rests in a substantial manner (**substantialiter**) (**De Princip.** II. 6, 6).

In this case also a theory of a purely moral unity has been attributed to Origen and he has been branded as a precursor of Nestorianism. But here too this is unjustifiable: "the unity thus established in Christ (is) meant as a genuine **ontological** unity."[16] For later readers, Origen's explanations are misleading, because he operated with presuppositions other than those later in use: when there is later mention of the human nature which is united with the person of the Word, that "nature" is conceived of as a thing, which is before it works; for Origen, that which is proper and spiritual in human nature is consciousness and freedom. By saying that this human nature is totally taken up in the Son and totally filled with him, Origen wanted to give expression to a genuine absolute, an ontological oneness: "the perfect and utmost participation in the Word-Itself, Wisdom-Itself, Justice-Itself" (**C. Celsum** V. 39; **De Princip.** IV. 4, 4), which surpasses in divine measure every union of men with God (**C. Celsum** II. 9).

This dynamic conception of being-an-image and this active presentation of the union of the humanity of Christ with the Word has the advantage that the complete human reality in Christ is brought into full light. In Jesus the absolutely highest union with the Son is realized as a conscious and loving union. Perfect vision of God and love are not here, as in later classic presentations of the incarnation, a consequence of the hypostatic union: they are the union itself in its highest point, in knowing and loving. As soon as this vision is torn loose from the broader context of Origen's vision of the image as being dynamic and active, as soon therefore as a distinction is made between the being and the activity of man, then this unity is reduced to a purely moral one.

In order to avoid this danger, Origen did not have at his disposal, as did Tertullian and his later Latin disciples, a technical terminology. We find the word **substantialiter** only in a text which is preserved in translation,[16a] and which can thus be a clarification on the part of the translator. But the less technical formulae, which we find in Irenaeus and Tertullian, return also in Origen. He repeatedly speaks about the "unification" through which the man Jesus is one reality with the Word (e.g., **C. Celsum** II. 9; V. 39). After his incarnation Jesus is a "composite something" (**C. Celsum** I. 66), so that there are in him not "two someones, but only one" (**Comm. Jo.** I. 28; **C. Celsum** VI. 47), namely, "God the Word who is man"

(Comm. Jo. XXXII. 25). The man in Jesus is "the same with himself" (ibid.), and that in a substantial manner (Comm. Jo. I. 28). Origen thus undoubtedly means that in Jesus, the divine Son and the man are the same subject—in later terminology: one person. That is abundantly clear from the manner in which he attributes human qualities to the Son of God and divine ones to the man.

In this vision Jesus is really the revelation of the Father. The Son indeed reflects in loving likeness the heart of the Father, and the man Jesus reflects in his turn the Son and thus ultimately the Father. In his human form and his human love and mercifulness, the interior of the Son appears which itself images the interior of the Father. And at the same time the ideal of man becomes clear in Jesus' humanity: that man exists and is alive who clings to God with all the fibers of his essence and thus realizes the essential kernel of human existence. This is a great and fundamentally orthodox vision of the incarnation and redemption.

But this vision is not free from dangers which we must briefly mention. The conception that the Son is the Image of the Father can lead, on one hand, to regarding the Son only as an apparition and as an apparent image of the Father: the distinction between the divine persons is then imperfectly maintained.

This potential development of Origen's thought does appear in a Marcellus of Ancyra (d. ca. 374); but nonetheless it could no longer be truly dangerous. On the other hand, the Son's being-an-image can be explained as an otherness and an inferiority in nature: in Platonic image theory there is a tendency "to consider the image as a degraded copy and an enfeeblement of the model."[17] Just how far Origen himself goes in this direction is disputed; in Arius (d. ca. 336) and also in Eusebius of Caesarea (d. ca. 339) and his followers, this inferiority of the image is developed into a system.

Origen's schema of image Christology can also lead to a violation of Jesus' humanity. If the only purpose of this humanity is to be a means of the appearance of the divine Word, then a human soul can seem to be superfluous. Why could not the body directly be the manifestation of the Word which is expressing itself in it, as, in other men, the soul expresses itself in the body? In Origen himself, this danger was overcome by his active conception of the image: because the image is a contemplating and loving likeness, the human knowledge and will of Jesus play a vital role in Origen's theory, and the spiritual soul forms an indispensable link between the Word and corporality. But as soon as this active conception of image begins to wane, the danger

threatens that the soul will be considered as superfluous or even as a hindrance to the unity of the
Word with the corporality. Arius and Eusebius of
Caesarea, with their conception of the Word as a
mediate being between God and creatures, are not
the only ones who come to a denial of the human
soul in Jesus. They are joined by such forceful defenders of the true divinity as Malchion (268) and
Apollinaris of Laodicea (d. ca. 390). And the orthodox defenders of Jesus' soul see themselves forced to
seek an argument outside the image theory and
outside the Word-Christology.

This danger in Origen's thought was even more
heightened by the fact that he laid no bridge between
his image-Christology and the traditional teaching
about the sacrifice of the cross. We heard him say
that in this sacrifice, the Word is the high priest,
and the humanity the (passive) victim. According
to his own image theory, the high-priestly deed of
the Word would have to reflect itself in an active
sacrificial relationship on the part of the man Jesus.
But Origen does not seem to have been aware of
this consequence of his own thought. The result is
that Jesus' human activity in the work of redemption
plays, in the strict sense, no essential role. With this
the Monophysitism and the Monotheletism of later
centuries already loom on the horizon.

Finally there is in this image theory the threat of a peculiar flight from Jesus' human activity and being. For the Christian Platonist, which Origen is, the true reality is the divine. The material and the bodily has meaning only insofar as it is the expression and the shadow of the divine.[18] But then Jesus' human activity has in itself no consistency and is irrelevant for our salvation, unless as a form for the appearance of spiritual relationships. Naturally Origen does not go so far because he is too strongly bound by tradition and Church violently to force his Christology and his teaching on the redemption into his image theory. And yet his preference leads toward a spiritual explanation, not only of the Old Testament but also of the New Testament: as the history of the Old Testament is a prefiguration of Jesus, so Jesus' earthly life and activity is a type, a shadow thus of spiritual and heavenly realities: "the body of Jesus (and especially his resurrection) . . . seem to me to be a prefiguration of the Church" (**Comm. Jo.** X. 35).[19] This is a deep and enriching thought, but one in which there is lurking danger that the facts and deeds of salvation will be evaporated into parables, the danger that the corporal will be consumed in the blaze of the divine.

This tendency was too obviously in conflict with the Catholic realism of the incarnation for it to be

able to have positive results. But the resistance
against it, with a tendency toward an exaggerated
accentuation of and an insistence upon the independence of the human in Jesus, is one of the motives
which inspires Paul of Samosata (268) and the school
of Antioch and which will lead to Nestorianism. And
in a remarkable manner, this Nestorianism, which
was inspired by the aim of resisting Origenism, will
still be able to appeal to Origen's thought for its
own support: the emphasis on human freedom and
consciousness in the union of the human with the
Word could seem to be a support for Nestorious'
theory of moral unity. Origen's christological thought
will form a wealthy source of inspiration for the
coming centuries in their reflection on the mystery
of the God-man. But it is also loaded with dangers
which come to light as soon as men of lesser vision
and spirit take over Origen's propositions without
adopting his broader vision. The later christological
debates concerning the true divinity and the true
humanity of Jesus already play against the background of Origen's reflections. And the Church will
avoid the dangers which lurk in these conceptions
only because she reaches back to Irenaeus' vision of
unity and to the formal, static christological schema
of Tertullian.

II

THE GREAT DEBATES
AND DEFINITIONS

Around the middle of the third century the foundations of the later christological development were laid. In the great centers of the Church, in Asia Minor and Gaul, in Rome and North Africa and Egypt, faith in Christ has acquired a form of expression which has been more or less rounded off. Jesus of Nazareth is someone of divine order, God's Son in an eminent sense, and he was born as man from Mary, lived as man and died and rose. In spite of this contrast in manner of existence and characteristics, he is one and the same. This fundamental insight of faith bears every further development; and all discussions will play themselves out in principle within this framework. Likewise in the same period the seeds of these debates and discussions are sown: namely, differing visions of the saving work of Christ begin to take shape, visions which are going to give a certain color to the fundamental convictions about the person of Christ, visions because of which these convictions may possibly be misformed. There is the vision of Irenaeus with its strong interest in the human

activity of Jesus, through which the sins of men are
made good. There is the vision of Origen, who sees
in Jesus' humanity above all the appearance of divine
realities. There is finally also the vision (or lack of
a vision) of Tertullian, who makes scarcely any connection between Jesus' person and his saving work,
and who thus inclines toward a static-formal analysis
of the constitution of the God-man.

One could nearly deduce a priori the later developments of the christological dogma: first Christ's
true and perfect divinity was defined (Council of
Nicaea, 325): indeed a thorn in the side of all those
who believed in the transcendent majesty and inac-
cessibility of the one and only God; and was not the
Hellenic conception of inferior divine beings a way
out? Thereafter it was defined that Jesus is true
and perfect man (Council of Constantinople, 381): not
only those who considered Jesus to be a demigod,
but also some of the fiery defenders of Nicaea who
regard his humanity as deified, are inclined to blend
his humanity with his heavenly nature. After both
poles of Jesus' essence were thus established, the
nature of their union was brought to discussion:
although true God and true man, he is still one and
the same (Council of Ephesus, 431), and in this union
neither his divinity nor his humanity is violated
(Council of Chalcedon, 451). With this, the formal

constitution of the God-man was completely defined. But precisely because the interest in these discussions was continually directed toward Christ's formal constitution, it appeared necessary safely to establish the principle of his true human life and action: Jesus has, in addition to the divine, also a truly human principle of operation and a true human will (Third Council of Constantinople, 680-681). During this same period, although not in express conciliar definitions, the insight has matured that Jesus is perfect and complete man, not in spite of but precisely because of the fact that he is God: he is the divinized man, and therefore man in a divine manner and in divine truth. With these last two declarations the fullness of the original vision of Irenaeus was rediscovered, the vision in which Jesus' saving work rested upon his genuinely human obedience, the vision of which it could be written: "Christ is perfect man simply because he is God."[20]

This logical schema of the development does truly correspond to the historical order of occurrence. But that does not in any way mean that the factual development consistently followed this schema. This is quite apparent, for example, from the fact that hardly any documents were preserved from the First Council of Constantinople: a sign that the men of that time did not perceive the importance of the

Council's declaration. The definition of the perfect humanity of Christ which was approved at Constantinople did not immediately meet with a full response within the Church, and only came to its rights in the discussion which led from Ephesus to Chalcedon. The older definition of Christ's full humanity was fully honored for the first time only after the solemn proclamation of Ephesus concerning the unity of the God-man. This unavoidably brings with it a certain lack of clarity concerning the Ephesian definition: How can there be a satisfactory discussion of unity if one of the two poles is imperfectly established? This lack of clarity surrounding Ephesus reflected itself in inextricable historical complications and in a semantic chaos in which the most serious dogmatic oppositions deteriorated into a conflict which had apparently to do only with words and concepts.

There are still other factors at the base of the factual precedence of Ephesus over Constantinople: church politics and theological differences and the rivalries between the Christian capital cities of the East—Alexandria, on one side; Antioch and, later, Constantinople, on the other. Thanks to the genius of Origen, Alexandria theologically had a tremendous lead on its rival in Syria. Through Athanasius' heroic fidelity to the faith and also through his powerful and aggressive politics, this advantage was enormously

strengthened. Antioch, on the contrary, was divided
and crippled through endless schisms throughout the
entire fourth century. Thus the Council of Constantinople did not have an immediate impact: it was in
Chalcedon that Constantinople achieved victory for
the first time. Another important factor in the christological struggle was the wrestling over leadership
in Alexandria and thus over the fundamental theological vision of Origen. The prestige of Alexandria
and of the moderate Origenism of the Alexandrian
church is one of the reasons why the unity of the
God-man could for so long a time remain a step
ahead of his real humanity. Thus the conflict concerning the christological dogma became a nearly
inextricable intermingling of dogmatic and theological
positions, of Church and state politics, and even of
personal tensions and rivalries.

1. A Preview: The Synod of Antioch in 268

The preview of the great struggle that would hold
Church and state in unrest for nearly a century took
place in a little known Synod which was held in
Antioch in the year 268 and which led to the condemnation and exile of the bishop of the city, Paul
of Samosata. We do not have much information
about the exact procedure of the discussions, but
thanks to a study by H. de Riedmatten, O.P.[21] we are
able to form a sufficient picture of the spiritual forces

which stood in opposition to each other and of the
significance of the conflict for the whole coming
century.

a. Paul of Samosata

Bishop Paul of Samosata was accused of an un-
christian way of life and of error. He was apparently,
scarcely ten years after Origen's death, a bitter anti-
Origenist, as is clear in his rejection of Origen's
formulae such as "two gods,"[22] "composition" of the
incarnate Word (fr. 22), visible appearance of the
Word in the flesh (fr. 12=28). According to Paul,
Jesus was an ordinary man: "Mary has not given birth
to the Word" but to "a man equal to us" (fr. 1, 4).
The man Jesus differs only in degree from the other
saints (fr. 31), namely, due to the fact that he is more
abundantly filled with God's grace than they (fr. 5)
and that the divine Wisdom dwells in him as in her
temple, even more than in Moses (fr. 7, 8, 31). But
the union between the divine Wisdom and the man
Jesus is a unity of instruction and of companionship
(fr. 33), of friendship (fr. 24), of quality (fr. 29). Thus
Jesus is the adopted Son of God. The divine Word
and the man Jesus are "one and another" (fr. 7).
But when his opponents reproached him for thus
distinguishing two sons in Christ (fr. 32), Paul forcefully protested (fr. 17, 21). Apparently this must be
explained by the fact that for Paul the divine Wisdom

of the Word is not an independent divine person, but only an attribute or energy of the Father, so that no immanent divine Son exists (fr. 13): it is only by means of the incarnation that the Word becomes Son.

The background of Paul's teaching is not completely clear. Certainly opposition to Origen plays a role. Another factor was probably Paul's desire to preserve the complete human reality of Jesus intact (against Origen's flight?): the man has suffered and given us life (fr. 11). There was probably also Paul's concern that, by truly becoming man, the divine Word would undergo a change (fr. 25, 29), and that thus a being of divine order, yes God himself, would become subject to change, birth, suffering, and death.

This teaching of Paul of Samosata will be revived again for a moment in Fontinus (ca. 340); and on some points Nestorianism will manifest some resemblance to it. Paul may probably serve as both a symptom and an extreme representative of one intellectual position, which a century later will surface in the school of Antioch. This school will be distinguished by an anti-Origenist proposition, by a strong emphasis on the true humanity of Jesus, and in its attempt to preserve this humanity intact, by a tendency to see only a relatively loose bond between the divinity and the humanity in Jesus. It is in this Antiochene school that Nestorianism will be born. As a symptom,

then, the appearance of Paul is important because
it warns of the presence in the Church of a current
which is set against the emphasis on the unity of the
God-man. In the fourth century this current will
scarcely come to the surface, but it still makes clear
the reason why the theme of the unity of the God-man
will temporarily be a step ahead of that of the true
humanity.

b.   Malchion

The reflections of Paul's opponents, on the contrary, represent the unity theory, and also bring to
light the dangers present in this, dangers which
temporarily do not seem to be recognized by the
leading figures of the Church and which thus remain
present as a temptation for a long time. Before Paul
was summoned before the Synod, six bishops made
an attempt to get him to alter his position. In their
letter they jointly summarize their faith in the God-
man as follows:

> The Son, who as God is with the Father,
> and who is Lord over all creation, was sent
> by the Father from heaven and became flesh
> and was made man. Therefore the flesh which
> was born from the Virgin is united without
> change to the divinity and is divinized. For
> these reasons, the same Jesus Christ foretold
> as God and as man in the Law and the
> Prophets, and believed in in the church. . . .

> He is one and the same according to his
> substance (**ousia**) even if he is known under
> differing aspects (**epinoiai**).[23]

At the Synod itself and in the synodal Proceedings,
of which only fragments are preserved, the matter
was gone into more deeply. Paul was accused of
dividing Christ in two (fr. 14, 19). No, Christ is one
and the same (fr. 18, 19, 23). For the very substance
of the Word is substantially in the man Jesus: the
word **ousia,** which we translate for the sake of brevity
as "substance" returns in many variations to charac-
terize the unity (fr. 14, 16, 22-24, 29, 33); it comes
from the verb "to be" and thus expresses that the
Word not only is united with the man Jesus through
his activity and power, but through his "being," on
the level of the very "being" of this man.

The Word-become-man is a composite something
(fr. 22, 25, 26) and man is a part of that composite
(fr. 14, 25, 36). One can thus compare the unity
between the Word and the man with that between
soul and body (fr. 30). And yet the bishops stoutly
maintain that the Word has undergone no change in
becoming man (fr. 25). So one can and must say that
the eternal Word was born, that he has suffered
weariness and hunger (fr. 18, 19, 23) and that, on
the other hand, the Wise Men from the East have
prayed to the human body which was filled with

God (fr. 15). But if they thus persistently posit the exchange of properties, they still make a distinction between the things which pertain primarily to God and secondarily to the man, and vice versa (**prohêgoumenôs, kata deteron logon**):

> God who has taken on the human thus shared in the suffering which is primarily human; and the human, in which God was and through which he accomplished his works, shared in the works which are primarily divine. In the womb (of Mary) he was formed primarily as man, and secondarily in the womb God became one substance with the human (fr. 34; cf. fr. 15, 20).[24]

One can only admire the maturity of the christological vision which is expressed in these fragments. Full of reminiscenes of Origen's formulations, these texts offer a very balanced summary of the faith in Christ. But nonetheless it will become apparent that it is dangerous to speak about the incarnate Word as about a "composite something"; nor is the comparison with the union between soul and body without objections: if the divine Word can enter into a genuine composition with something created, is it then still totally divine? The comparison with the union between body and soul will in the course of the centuries return time and again. It can mean that the Word is the ultimate subject even of Jesus' human existence, as in man the soul is the ultimate subject even of his physical life. But it could also mean that the Word takes over the place of the human soul; then the full humanity of Jesus is insufficiently preserved, and the genuine divinity of the Word is also violated. Precisely which of these two meanings the bishops of Antioch attributed to this comparison cannot be determined; but their spokesman and trusted agent seems to have had the latter meaning in mind. The priest Malchion had, on behalf of the Synod, the task of convincing Paul of Samosata of his error. This Malchion says that the constitution of Jesus differs from our own, "through the fact that in him the God-Word is what in us the interior man (the soul) is" (fr. 30). And he asks Paul whether, "as we men are composed of flesh and someone who is in the flesh, is it also thus that the living Substance, the Word itself and the Wisdom itself was in that body? . . . As in us (life) consists in this composition, so also (life consists) in him in the fact that the God-Word and what is from the Virgin conjoin in the same" (fr. 36).

Malchion seems truly to have been convinced that the divine Word is not only the final subject of Jesus' bodily life but also its vital principle, and thus that the Word takes the place of the human soul. Apparently he arrives at this because he fears that a human soul in Jesus would be a "second Someone" in addition to the Word. But it is especially here that he takes revenge upon the one-sidedness of Origenism, which saw in Jesus only a bodily appearance of the Word and had no need for an authentic human operation and existence in the Lord. Origen himself had preserved the human soul of Jesus for the sake of his dynamic conception of the image. In Malchion and in all the later Origenists this vision of "being-an-image" was lost; then a human soul becomes superfluous and even disturbing for the vision of the unity of the incarnate Word. The necessity of recognizing a human soul in Jesus will only come to be recognized in the circle of Origen's followers when attention is again drawn to the other aspects of Jesus' work of salvation.

Malchion's standpoint is therefore very important, because it represents the second currents which will remain for yet a century. Pamphylus must defend Origen against the accusation that he divided the Lord in two by accepting a human soul in Christ (**Apol. Pro Origene** 5, **PG** 17, 590A; cf. 579A). Eusebius of Caesarea, the disciple of Pamphylus, will expressly deny this human soul in Christ.[25] Arius apparently also did that; the Arian standard-bearers from the middle of the fourth century certainly did so.[26] Around 360 this current will come to the surface when Apollinaris of Laodicea, a faithful supporter of Athanasius and a dedicated defender of Nicaea, makes the denial of the human soul in Christ the central point of his Christology. These instances do not stand isolated from one another, but manifest the presence of this theory even within ecclesiastical circles. One confirmation of this lies in the fact that for the time being only the voice of Eustathius of Antioch (ca. 330) is raised against this theory, while Athanasius and even Cyril of Alexandria in the first years of his career scarcely become excited about this.

To us hesitation on this point seems incomprehensible: is not the denial of a human soul in Christ the same as a denial of the incarnation? For these authors this is apparently not the case, for all of them are eager to preserve the true incarnation. But they seem to have been of the opinion that man does not have to be defined as a union of a human soul and a body, but as that of a spirit (of whatever nature) and a body: so in their eyes Christ, the Word which had taken on a body, was thus genuinely and unreservedly man: "Any spiritual being that imprisons itself in a body can be said to 'become man,' because it is an incarnate spirit."[27] We cannot go deeper into the question of whether or to what degree Athanasius and Cyril themselves ignored or neglected a human soul in Christ.[28]

It is, rather, the phenomenon itself that is of the utmost importance, because it points to a development of the doctrine of redemption and Christology in a definite direction. In Irenaeus any hesitation on this point was ruled out, because in his vision of the incarnation and redemption, the human will and freedom of Christ, who destroyed in divine-human obedience the disobedience of Adam, played a major role. A denial or neglect of Jesus' human soul is possible only when the redemption is conceived of as an activity of the divine Word in which the human remains purely passive. One example of this, as Cyril of Alexandria will himself later remark, is when the redemption is reduced to an appearance of the Word among men (**De recta fide ad Theodosium** 19, **ACO** I. 1/1, pp. 53f.). Another example would be when, in the sacrifice of the cross, one places all the activities in the divine Word, who fulfills the function of high priest, and sees in Jesus' humanity only the passive victim. And, despite several declarations to the contrary by Athanasius (**Or. c. Arian** II. 8), this is for the time being the generally accepted mode of conception: only Cyril will emphasize that Jesus is high priest precisely as having become man.

If one does not see the necessity of a humanly free activity in the work of the redemption, it is difficult to affirm the reality of a human soul in

Jesus. In the Alexandrian milieu of Athanasius and Cyril and their supporters, another principle will be appealed to for help, a principle which for this reason will gain a heavy emphasis and will become one of the great pillars of the Greek doctrine of redemption and of Christology: **What the Word has not taken on is not redeemed** or, worded positively, **The Word redeems what it takes on and by taking it on.**

We will consider the development of this principle from the very beginning. There are several authors who have remarked that this is a variance of the older "exchange" principle, that the Son became what we are in order to make us what he is (e.g., Irenaeus, **Adv. Haer. V. Praef.**: cf. above p. 14). But in the exchange theory the emphasis lay on the fact that the Son became a child of Adam, who came under the law of suffering and death and who made us God's children, who in turn approach to the Father with him: the exchange then was related to the entire human life from conception up to and including death. Here, however, the emphasis is upon the acceptance of a human body and a human soul and thus upon the first moment of the incarnation.

2. **Christ's True Divinity and the Development of the Principle: What the Word Has Not Taken On Is Not Redeemed**

a. Arius

Arius, the priest of Alexandria (d. **ca.** 336), is
certainly linked with the Antiochene teacher Lucian,
and so possibly also with the above-mentioned
Malchion.[29]

It is possible that Arius also denied that Christ
has a human soul; certainly his most important disciples did this.[30] It is even possible that precisely
the theories of Malchion brought him to his characteristic teaching about Christ's divinity: if the Word
actually can become the immanent vital principle of
the human body and thus enter into a composition,
then the divine cannot be complete. Whatever there
may be to this, his contemporaries almost exclusively
found in Arius the denial of Christ's divinity, and thus
it is on this point that his significance for the development of dogma is based. Although Arius continues
to give the name "god" to the Son, he does not
recognize in him a truly divine being. The Son
stands high above ordinary creatures, but still below
the Father. For the Son is himself a creature. He
is indeed not unbegotten, but he was begotten: and
begotten neither of the substance of the Father,
which indeed is indivisible, nor from any other element, and thus was begotten from nothing. Therefore, although created before all ages, he is still not
eternal. It is in this way that Arius presented his

theory to his fellow student of Lucian, who will shortly become his convinced supporter and later his most influential defender, Bishop Eusebius of Nicomedia:

> The Son was not begotten of, nor is he a part of the Unbegotten . . . , nor did he come to be from any element, but through the will and decision (of God) he received existence before time and before the ages, "full of grace and truth, god, only-begotten, without change." And before he was brought forth . . . he was not: for he is not unbegotten.
>
> We are accused because we have said: The Son has a beginning, but God is without beginning. . . . And: He is from nothing, because he indeed is not part of God nor of any element. . . .[31]

It is impossible and indeed for our purpose also superfluous to trace the course of the Arian controversy which for more than half a century would keep the Church of the East in endless confusion. But in the beginning of this controvesy, Bishop Alexander of Alexandria, supported by Ossius of Cordova and Emperor Constantine, succeeded at the Council of Nicaea (325) in gaining the condemnation of Arius and some of the most rabid of his followers. There also the dogma was defined which time and again in the following centuries would serve as the touchstone of orthodoxy:

> We believe . . . in one Lord Jesus Christ,
> the Son of God, begotten from the Father,
> only-begotten, that is from the substance of
> the Father, God from God, light from light,
> true God from true God, begotten not made,
> of one nature (**homoousios**) with the Father.
> . . . Who because of us men and because of
> our salvation came down and became incar-
> nate, becoming man, suffered and on the third
> day rose. . . .

> But as for those who say, "There was a
> time when he was not" and "Before he was
> brought forth, he was not" and "He came into
> existence out of nothing" or who claim that the
> Son of God is from a different hypostasis or
> substance (**ousia**) or is a creature or is subject
> to change—these the Catholic Church anathe-
> matizes (**DS** 125-126).[32]

In this Creed of Nicaea, great attention is paid to
the genuine divinity of the pre-existent Son. For us
it is of greater importance that this Son, whose divinity
is so forcefully declared, is nonetheless and without
any hesitation also described as the one who was
born from the virgin and who has lived and died.
It is abundantly and explicitly stated that this Jesus
Christ is one Lord and Son. One should not shirk
from the proclamation of the identity of the pre-
existent Son of God and the historical man Jesus of
Nazareth on the grounds that the sufferings of his

human existence and death belonged to the most eloquent arguments against Jesus' true divinity.

b. Athanasius

The definition of Nicaea came to be of decisive importance for the development of Christology. But it would take nearly fifty years before the definition was commonly accepted. For almost half a century Athanasius, who became Bishop of Alexandria in 328, had to lead an uninterrupted and often lonely struggle against the united power of the Arians and other opponents of Nicaea. In this controversy, Athanasius became the beacon of Nicene orthodoxy and for succeeding generations her oracle. The various ways in which he treated of the doctrine of redemption and Christology in this debate thus came to exercise a widespread influence.

Even before the outbreak of the Arian controversy, the young deacon Athanasius had ventured into a "precociously youthful excursion into high theology"[33] in a work of which two books are known to us under the titles **Against the Pagans** and **Concerning the Incarnation of the Word.**[34] In these works he shows himself to be an industrious disciple of Origen as well as of Irenaeus. From the former he borrowed his vision on the situation in paradise and the Fall and on the redemption as being God's revelation:

man, created according to God's Image and living
from the vision of God, has turned away from God
(**De Incarn.** 39). He can be saved only because the
eternal Image of God appears in bodily form (**De
Incarn.** 13-14).

The influence of Irenaeus is much stronger. By
departing from Life, man has condemned himself to
death. Life can be given to him only owing to the
fact that he who is Life nestles in our mortal body
(**De Incarn.** 44), and descends unto our death (**De
Incarn.** 9). Through this sacrifice of his death, he
redeems our debt of death (**De Incarn.** 8).

A comparison with Irenaeus' doctrine of redemption would be especially interesting, but we can only
refer to two points: less emphasis on the descent of
Jesus into the complete human life, more on his
death which is explicitly described as a sacrifice;
and especially a revival of the exchange theory without
the characteristic Irenaean motif of recapitulation but
in several variations. Athanasius himself, for example,
summarized his work as follows:

> He became man in order that we could
> become deified. He has revealed himself
> through a body in order that we could learn
> to know the invisible Father. He has born the
> indignity on the side of men (namely by allow-
> ing himself to be killed), in order that we could
> inherit immortality (**De Incarn.** 54).

Forty years later Athanasius writes: "He accepted
what is proper to us (namely suffering and death)
and destroyed this by offering it as a sacrifice, and
thus clothed us with what is proper to him" (**Ad
Epictetum** 6).

Athanasius' importance for Christology consists in
this rediscovery of Irenaeus and of the exchange
theory, and in the influence which this theory ac-
quires through the personal authority of the Bishop
of Alexandria, and through the exceptional place
which it takes in his teaching on the Trinity.

In the controversy concerning the true divinity of
the Son, one of Athanasius' recurrent arguments is:
Only the Creator himself can re-create man (**Ad
Adelphium** 8; cf. **De Incarn.** 7) and especially: Only
the true God can deify us:

> If the Son were a creature man would . . .
> not have come into contact with God. For a
> creature would not have brought creatures into
> contact with God, because it in turn would
> itself need someone who effects this contact.
> Nor could an element of creation have been
> the salvation of creation, because it itself had
> also to be saved (**Contra Arianos** II. 69).[35]

The old exchange principle that "God became
man in order to deify us" (**C. Arian.** I. 38; **Ad Adelph.**
4), or as he once states, in order "to make [us] into

the Word" (**C. Arian.** III. 33),[36] thus serves in Athanasius as an argument for Jesus' true divinity: he deifies us, therefore he must be truly God. But he must also be truly and completely man. That is indeed the reverse side of the exchange theory, as Athanasius himself understood:

> Therefore let those who deny that the Son stems by nature from the Father . . . , also deny that he truly has taken on human flesh from the ever-virgin Mary. For it would be of equally little use to us men if he did not truly become flesh, as if the Word was not truly and by nature the Son of God (**C. Arian.** II. 70).

Therefore Athanasius continually emphasized that our Savior had to be born from Adam's race so that he is related to us. Jesus as man is the firstborn and eldest brother of regenerated mankind, the principle of our renewal. Nor does Athanasius hesitate to stamp Jesus' humanity as "redeemed," an expression toward which later theology will at times be quite cold:

> His flesh was the first saved and liberated, because it was the body of the Word himself. And since that time we also, because we have the same body, (or: because we form one body: **sussômoi**), are saved because of this" (**C. Arian.** II. 61; cf. III. 22).

This reverse side of the exchange theory will help Athanasius to establish his standpoint when, toward the end of his life, the denial of Jesus' human soul comes to the fore. At the Alexandrian Synod of 362, Athanasius summarizes his doctrine of redemption and Christology against the old error of Paul of Samosata and the new error of Apollinaris in the following decree:

> The Word of the Lord did not dwell in the holy man in the same way which He came into the prophets . . . but the Word himself became flesh. And he who is in God's form, took the form of a slave and was born as man according to the flesh from Mary for our sake. Thus in him the human race was perfectly and completely freed from sins, brought to life from the dead, and led into the kingdom of heaven.

> The Redeemer did not have a body that was inanimate or non-emotional or non-rational. For because the Lord became man for our sake, it was impossible that his body be non-rational, and in the Word took place the salvation not only of the body but also of the soul.

> And he who was truly God's Son became also the Son of man; and the same who was the only-begotten Son of God, became also the firstborn among many brothers. Therefore it was not one who was before Abraham and another who came to be after Abraham; nor was it one who awakened Lazarus and another

who inquired after him; but the same said
humanly: Where is Lazarus lying? and divinely awakened him ... (**Tomus ad Antiochenos** 7).

For Athanasius the most important element remained the identity between the eternal Son of God
and the man Jesus. Due to the fact that the Son
took on a human "nature" (Athanasius did not yet
use the word "nature" in this sense) and thus from
that point on a man from our race is the Son of God,
the salvation of the family of man and its reunion
with God is a fact. This identity of the subject does
not remove the necessity of distinguishing between
what comes to him on the grounds of his being
God and what on the grounds of his being man.
Moreover, Athanasius had already emphasized this
distinction in his polemic against the Arians, who
denied the true divinity of Christ on the grounds of
his human weaknesses.

The new development in the above text is in the
second paragraph, although this modification is introduced somewhat hesitantly. This document aims at
a reconciliation between the different followers of
Nicaea, among whom were also the moderate Apollinarians. Their opponents undoubtedly accused them
as follows: By denying Jesus' human soul, you make
him into an inanimate and nonrational body. All
parties easily agreed that this was absurd. But the

Apollinarians were of the opinion that Jesus' body was animated and rational because it was filled with the Word himself. The first lines still leave room for this interpretation: if the Word himself takes on a body, it must be a completely "rational" body. But the closing words of the paragraph are certainly directed against Apollinaris: through the incarnation both body and soul were saved, and since this salvation was realized by being taken on by the Word, Jesus' humanity cannot be "inanimate" and "non-rational" including the sense that he takes on a rational soul.[37] The same theory was expressed by Athanasius in a dogmatic letter of the same period:

> Because the Redeemer actually and truly became man, the whole man was saved. . . . Our salvation is no illusion, nor is it limited to the body alone, but in the Word himself was truly effected the salvation of the whole man, of soul and of body (**Ad Epict.** 7)[38]

In the condemnation of his old adversary, Apollinaris, Athanasius demonstrates great moderation. One of the consequences of this mildness will be that Cyril of Alexandria, the inheritor of his spirit, will not always be sufficiently on the alert for the erroneous unity theory of Apollinaris. But it remains certain that, through his adaptation of the exchange theory to the new problem, Athanasius made a decisive contribution to the development of the princi-

ple which shortly will become a classic pillar of
Christology and which will be formulated by Gregory
of Nazianzus in these words: "What is not taken on
(by the Word) is not healed; but what is united with
God is also saved" (**Ep.** 101 **ad Cledonium, PG** 37,
181f.).

This principle shattered the impasse into which
the semi-Origenism of Malchion had fallen: if one
takes a one-sided view of the incarnation as the bodily
appearance of the Word, the human soul of Jesus
becomes superfluous or even damaging. From now
on the response to this will be to say with Athanasius
that the soul also had to be taken on, because the
soul was also in need of salvation. Certain characteristics of this adaptation of the exchange theory must
briefly be pointed out. In the first place, an excess
of the Origenist image theory is here corrected with
the aid of a principle that is borrowed from a totally
different vision of the incarnation; this obviously
cannot be conducive to harmony in christological
thought. Further, the stress in the doctrine of the
incarnation and the redemption is placed on the conception, thus on the moment of the incarnation and
not on the entire life of the God-man. As a result,
all the attention is concentrated on the fact that the
Son of God becomes and is a complete man; but the
importance of the fact that he also acts as complete

man continues to be little appreciated. In the work of redemption, the divine Son is active and his humanity is passive: this humanity is taken on, sanctified, and offered up to the Father as victim. That this humanity also lovingly accepts its new being, that it also sanctifies itself by the power of the Word (cf. John 17:18), and that anointed by the Spirit it also offers itself up (cf. Heb. 9: 14)—all of this is ignored in this vision. In this theory, thus, the human principle of operation and the human freedom in Jesus play no role. This shortcoming in the vision of Athanasius and his disciples apparently contributed greatly to provoking the counter-reaction of the Antiochene school and accounted in part for the stubbornness of the Nestorian resistance against Ephesus and even against Chalcedon.

3. The Controversy over Unity: From Constantinople to Ephesus

The decisive controversy about the unity of the God-man did not break out in Alexandria, but in the neighborhood of Antioch. Until now this unity had scarcely become a problem: the old formulae were generally repeated that the Word of God and the man Jesus were not one and another, but one and the same. According to the Johannine vision, which was passed on and explained by Origen, Jesus of Nazareth was thought to be no other than the eternal Word

which became flesh and appeared among us. Only
Paul of Samosata had contested this conviction, but
his conception of Jesus as the most perfect of the
prophets in whom the Word of God rested was too
strongly in conflict with the Gospel picture to be a
serious danger. Paul of Samosata did not have a
direct influence on the controversy that broke out a
century after his condemnation; but his adversary,
Malchion, apparently did have such an influence on
the controversy. And it is certainly no accident that
the controversy broke out in Antioch where anti-
Origenist forces had long been at work.

Around the year 360 in Antioch two parties formed
in opposition to one another: one regarded the unity
in Christ more loosely; the other exaggerated this
unity to the extreme. The debate between these two
became significant for the history of the world, for
the formulations of the Councils of Ephesus and of
Chalcedon reflect the influences of each of these
groups. Just who set the spark to the powder is not
clear. In Antioch there was a current of thought
which emphasized the humanity more than Athanasius
had done. And Apollinaris, who pictured himself as
the exponent of the pure thought of Athanasius in
the area of Antioch, felt himself obliged to proclaim
and systematize his thoughts. In so doing he was
goaded to extremes by his opponents. And his adver-

saries, Diodore of Tarsus at first and then Theodore
of Mopsuestia, felt themselves compelled to launch
a protest against this and to proclaim the complete
fullness of the humanity of Jesus. The aggressive-
ness of their disciple Nestorius again provoked resistance from Cyril of Alexandria who, through a fatal
misunderstanding, allowed himself to use Apollinarian
expressions. The developments of these years can
be summarized in three sections. Apollinaris' teaching and condemnation; the Antiochene school; Nestorius and Cyril.

a. Apollinaris and His Condemnation

Opinions concerning the condemnation of Apollinaris (d. ca. 390) are strongly divided. According to
Riedmatten[39] "he is essentially a Monophysite, possibly the only genuine Monophysite"; according to
others he is definitely not a Monophysite.[40] Whatever the case may be, there is relative agreement
concerning his teaching.

He wants to work out the old principle that the
Son-became-man actually is one and the same. He
is not "one and another"; nor is he two sons, one by
nature and the other through grace.[41] Apollinaris has
various expressions for this unity: the God-man is
one "person (**prosôpon**: fr. 4; **De unione** 10), one substance (**ousia**: fr. 9, 158), one nature (**physis**: fr. 10).

In this connection there is a formula, which, when adopted by Cyril, has fatal consequences: "The one Son is not two natures, the one adorable, the other not, but **one incarnate nature of the God-Word,** which, with its flesh is adored in one adoration" (**Ep. ad Jov.** pp. 250f.).

In addition to this, Apollinaris uses the traditional comparison: just as man, although composed of soul and body is still only one nature, so also the God-man is likewise one nature (**Ep. ad Dionys.** 2, p. 257).[42]

But this comparison does not here, as in Athanasius, mean only that the incarnate Son is the same "I." With Malchion, Apollinaris goes further; and this becomes the central point of his teaching: in this composite which the God-man is, the Word himself takes the place which the soul occupies in ordinary men. Or at least—in a sense Apollinaris wavered, conceivably under pressure from his adversaries—the Word takes the place of the higher soul, which in us is the seat of understanding and freedom, the chief principle of our human life, the **nous.** Christ has no human **nous** but in him its function is fulfilled by the Word himself: "Next to the soul (here to be understood as the lower soul, which is the principle of vegetative and sensitive life) and body, Christ has God as spirit, that is an **nous**" (fr. 25).

In both early and recent times great emphasis has been laid on the peculiar and closely Aristotelian anthropology of Apollinaris, which proceeds from the supposition that in man body and soul form one nature.

But the source and core of his teaching do not lie in this anthropology but, rather, in a conviction of faith. Apollinaris desires with all his strength to maintain that the Word of God and the man Jesus are one and the same, and that thus the Word himself has suffered for us and is risen. And according to him such a unity cannot consist of two substances, each of which is complete in itself and "finished" and thus in itself a principle of life (fr. 107): the Word himself must be the principle of Jesus' human life and activity. Jesus is thus not simply man as we are, but "like a man," "because he is not of one nature (**homoousios**) with men according to that which is most important in him" (fr. 45).

According to Apollinaris, this is what St. John wished to express when he wrote that the Word became flesh, without adding to this "and soul" (fr. 2). The higher soul in man is the principle, through which he is an autonomous someone and through which he stands before God as an other. Thus if Jesus had such a human soul, he would truly be an other.

It is not therefore as a philosophical principle
that this principle is the ultimate ground for Apollinaris' denial of the human soul in Christ. For him
it has a strictly religious significance. In order to
redeem the sinful family of man, Jesus must be the
absolute holy; but absolute sanctity is incapable of
existing where a human soul is the principle of life;
indeed only God is holy and all human freedom includes the possibility of sin. The sanctity of the
human soul is necessarily free (and God as Creator
does not violate the nature of things: fr. 87) and consequently accidental. Jesus' holiness, on the contrary,
is substantial: "the incarnation itself is the sanctifying
of the flesh" (**De Unione** 11, p. 190).

His holiness is not the result of "ascesis" (fr. 75);
he is also holy according to his flesh from the very
beginning:

> The Lord is correctly named a holy crea-
> ture from the beginning, also with respect to
> his body; and in this he differs from every
> other body. For he was received in his
> mother's womb not without the divinity but
> in union with it (**De Unione** 1, p. 185).

This demand for substantial holiness seems to be
for Apollinaris the essential ground for denying the
human soul in Christ. He returns to this point repeatedly:

[The will of God is sufficient to] enliven and move the flesh through the Word which dwells in it, through the fact that the divine power takes the place of the soul and of the human **nous**. . . . For it is impossible that two substances endowed with **nous** and will can come together in one, if one wishes to avoid that they come into conflict with each other through their own will and power. Thus the Word did not take on a human soul, but only the seed of Abraham (fr. 2; fr. 153).

The Word became flesh but did not take on a human **nous** which is subject to change and to impure thoughts. But it is itself a divine, unchanging, heavenly **nous** (**Ep. ad Diocaes.** 2, p. 256; cf. **Kata meros pistis** 30, p. 178).[43]

Apollinaris expressly presents himself with the dilemma: substantial holiness or voluntary holiness (**Anakeph.** 24f., p. 25). He chooses the first and sacrifices to this the full humanity of the Lord. A long series of proofs repeat as a refrain the conclusion: "This Christ is not a man" (**Anakeph.** 2-14, p. 243). He is God-man. The flesh which is animated by the Word is not in the proper sense a creature (fr. 153), it is one in substance (**homoousios**) with God (**De Unione** 8, p. 188), because it is blended into one substance with God (fr. 116).

Apollinaris thus goes essentially further than the

ordinary **communicatio idiomatum** (interchange of characteristics), according to which the characteristics of the divine and the human nature can be stated of the one God-man. For him there exists in Christ a true penetration of the divine characteristics in the humanity of the Lord. This is the meaning of the Apollinarian "one nature."[44]

His adversaries objected to two points in Apollinaris: his overexaggeration of the interchange of characteristics and in particular his denial of a human soul in Christ. Athanasius had already rejected these two points in 362.[45] This condemnation did not have any direct result. But after ten years came opposition from Epiphanius of Salamis, Ambrose, Gregory of Nazianzus, Gregory of Nyssa, Didymus the Blind, and others. New condemnations come from Roman synods under Pope Damasus and finally from the Council of Constantinople (381). In this polemic it was continually emphasized that Jesus is a complete and full man. A Roman Synod (369), later ratified by an Antiochene Synod, wrote as follows:

> We are amazed that some seem to think in an unorthodox manner about the Trinity, but not about the mystery of our redemption. For they contend that our Lord and Redeemer took on an incomplete man, namely one without understanding (**sensus=nous**). Alas, what a kinship with the Arians! For these latter

say that the divinity of the Son of God is incomplete, but the former that the humanity of the Son of man is incomplete. But if an incomplete man is taken on, then our salvation is incomplete, because the entire man is not saved. And what remains then of the word of the Lord: "I have come to save what was lost," namely the whole man, in soul and body, in understanding, and in the whole substance of his nature. . . . We know that we are completely and entirely saved, and confess therefore with the confession of the Catholic Church, that the complete God has taken on a complete man (**Mansi** III. 461; cf. also **Tomus Damasi, DS** 159).

The new form of the exchange principle, developed by Athanasius—that man is redeemed through the fact that the Son of God becomes man—touched a responsive chord, so that in a short time this view became commonly accepted. This argument was effective because, while passing over all the subtleties, it touched that point of Apollinarianism which was in direct conflict with the Catholic doctrine: is not the whole gospel filled with the wonderful message that Jesus, however holy and divine, still is truly a man like ourselves? But in this argument, the deeper question which Apollinaris had presented was scarcely touched upon, namely, how the full humanity in Jesus can conjoin with his true divinity,

and especially how his genuine human freedom can
be rhymed with his substantial sanctity. In the strong
orthodoxy which had formed itself around Athanasius,
there was still little eye for the mystery of Jesus'
human activity. The orthodox theologians remained
imprisoned in the proposition that in the work of
salvation, activity lies exclusively on the side of the
Word, while what is human in Jesus was conceived
of as being purely passive, or at the most of being
a passively moved **organon.** Jesus is seen to be the
man who radiantly comes forth from God and is
moved by him; it is not yet understood that he is
also the man who, raised by God, lives in a perfectly
human way toward the Father. Yet another century
will go by before this statement of the problem becomes a conscious one in the Church as a whole.

b. The Antiochene School: Two Natures

The school of Antioch paid greater attention to
the genuine humanity of the Lord. At least this is the
case insofar as any judgment can be made. For the
dogmatic writings of the most characteristic representatives of this school are preserved only in scarce
fragments, selected by their opponents, pulled out
of their context, and at times even falsified. Insofar
as the documents allow a judgment, one could say:
Athanasius employed as a favorite maxim "The Word
was made flesh," and he thus presupposes that the

Word is also in one way or another the subject of
the human existence of Jesus. But the Antiochene
formula should, rather, be: "Jesus is the man who
was filled and taken on by the Word." It is possible
that another proposition is echoed in this, in contrast
to the Scriptures; there may even be a very primitive
Syro-Palestinian tradition here. But for us, the phenomenon becomes clearly visible only in the fourth
century. And then it becomes apparent that the difference rests on a different approach taken in the
anti-Arian polemic. The fullness of Jesus' humanity
is stressed by the Antiochene school not directly
because of its significance for salvation, but in order
to defend the divinity of the Son.

This Antiochene tendency is already clearly dis-
cernible in Bishop Eustathius of Antioch (d. **ca.** 360)
who was one of the most prominent participants in
and faithful defenders of the Council of Nicaea.
Athanasius and his followers press the fight against
Arianism above all by studying the relationship of
the Word to the Father. But the polemic of Eustathius
directs itself preferably against the argument put
forward by the Arians: if the Son could be born of
the Virgin and suffer and die, then he is not truly
God (cf. fr. 15).[46] Thus he even goes so far as to make
a sharp distinction between the properties of the Son
and those of the man Jesus. This is nothing excep-

tional. But with this, Eustathius regularly sets in contrast to each other "The one who anoints" and "the one who is anointed" (fr. 35), the man who suffers and the God who dwells in him, who raised him up and glorifies him (fr. 37, 41, 47, 50). These differ in nature (fr. 41, 47) so that the weakness of the man does no violence to the majesty of God. When one recalls the frequency and insistence with which all the former generations had repeated that the Son of God and the man Jesus are not "one and another" but "one and the same," one is struck by the absence of such formulae, even by a manner of speaking which seems to see in the Son and the man almost "one and another" (although Eustathius does not use this expression).

It is in this that we find the specific character of the Antiochene description. The difference is not in the terms "the man taken on," "the man of Christ" (fr. 33), "organ" (fr. 23), or in the description of the unity as an indwelling (fr. 19, 20). These and like expressions and suppositions are also employed by Athanasius and his followers. But the background is different.

On the other hand, Eustathius naturally presupposes the unity of the Word of God and the man Jesus. As a faithful supporter of Nicaea he can speak of the two births of Christ (fr. 67), of the birth of

God from the Virgin (fr. 88), and thus also call Mary the Mother of God (fr. 68). But it was inevitable that this unity would become a problem in this framework of thought.

Diodore, later Bishop of Tarsus (d. ca. 390) was a teacher in Antioch around 360, thus in the same years that Apollinaris worked there. A heated polemic developed between these two. And in this struggle Diodore showed that he was a disciple of Eustathius. He did not explicitly direct himself against the denial of the human soul in Christ by Apollinaris, but against the fact that the "one nature" of the God-man necessarily led to attributing the human weakness of Jesus to the Son of God himself.[47] But Diodore was more systematic than Eustathius and went a (fatal) step further. He not only opposed Apollinaris' "one nature" and "one ousia"[48] but explicitly rejected the latter's teaching that the "body and the God-Word is the same, and not one and another, but a single composite . . . one single Son in both."[49]

Diodore thus denies that the Son of God is born of Mary: what she bore was the temple which the Son formed for himself in her womb, the man with whom he united himself. Only in this sense did he wish to accept the title "Mother of God."[50] Thus Diodore is reported to have taught that "the God-Word can be called the Son of David only in the

broad sense (**katachrêstikôs**=through an oversight).[51]
He wrote further:

> You will throw up to me: "Do you preach
> two sons?" No, I do not say that there are
> two sons of David; for I have not said, that
> the Son of God is the Son of David; but
> neither do I say that there are two, who
> according to their substance are the Son of
> God: for I have not said that there are two
> who are out of God's substance. But I say that
> the eternal God-Word has dwelt in him who
> was born from David's seed (**ibid.,** 1388A).

And also:

> The man who was born from Mary is the
> Son through grace, the God-Word is Son
> through nature. . . . It must be sufficient for
> the human body to possess sonship, glory,
> immortality through grace (**ibid.,** 1388A).

"Two sons"—this will be continually thrown in
the face of the Nestorians. And must the man Jesus
be called Son of God in nature or in grace? Or is
there a third possible answer, that through the uniting
grace he is the **natural** Son of God? Diodore here
exhibits more cleverness than the cautiousness which
is appropriate in treating of this mystery. The fragments of Diodore's work are too scarce and for the
most part too polemical to judge to what degree he
preserves the unity between the Son of God and the

Son of David. His significance and his fame lie in his two disciples, who belong among the greatest exegetes of all time: Chrysostom and Theodore.

Chrysostom (d. 407), the Antiochene priest who was raised to Patriarch of Constantinople by Emperor Arcadius and who was driven into death by the hatred of Empress Eudoxia and Patriarch Theophilus of Alexandria, was a disciple of Diodore. It is rather possible that the saint did not feet completely happy with Diodore's christological suppositions. For although he preached in the church of Antioch, which was torn by the Apollinarian conflict, Chrysostom avoided nearly all discussion of these problems. Even in his catechesis for those about to be baptized, he restricted himself to a few laconic sentences about the mystery of the God-man (**Hom. Cat.** 1, 21, **Source Chrét.** 50, p. 119).

On several occasions, though, he did introduce a small but important correction of his master. Thus he states in his commentary on John 1: 14:

> He says: "the Word became flesh" in order to show that it was no illusion; but "become" also signifies no change of his substance (**ousia**), but the taking on of a true flesh. . . . (Therefore the evangelist adds to this: "and he dwelt amongst us"). It is not a change of this unchangeable nature, but having-a-tent and indwelling. And that which dwells is not the

> same as the tent but something else. For the
> one dwells in the other. . . . "Something else"
> I said, according to the substance. For through
> the union and conjunction, the God-Word and
> the flesh are one something, not through mix-
> ture and destruction of the substances, but
> through an ineffable and inexpressible union
> (**Hom. in Jo.** 11, 2, **PG** 59, 79f.).

The Antiochene fear that "to become" would be
"to change" is dominant. But where Diodore would
have spoken of "another," Chrysostom uses the neuter
form, and adds to this the abundant clarification that
this "being-other" has a relation to the substance,
that is to say to what he is. More balanced than his
master, Chrysostom thus seeks to preserve both distinction and unity in the God-man. Thus in his
commentary on Phil. 2: 6 he states:

> Christ is not "purely a man." He was not
> only what was visible, but also God. For he
> was visible as man, but he was not alike to the
> mass of men, even though he was alike accord-
> ing to the flesh. . . . We are soul and body, he
> is God and soul and body. . . . Remaining what
> he was, he took what he was not, and while
> he became flesh, he remained what he is,
> God-Word. . . . Let us then not mix, but also
> not separate. One God, one Christ, the Son of
> God. If I say "one" I mean union, no mixture,
> as if the one nature became changed in the
> other, but it is united with it (**Hom. in Phil.**
> 7, 2-3, **PG** 62, 231-2).

Not mixture but union: What game of Providence allows Chrysostom to rediscover precisely the expression which Tertullian had once formulated and which will later become one of the building stones of Chalcedon?

Theodore of Mopsuestia (d. **ca.** 428), Chrysostom's friend and fellow student of Diodore, was and is one of the most bitterly contested figures in the history of dogma. After his death there were heavy attacks from Cyril of Alexandria, who saw in him the father of Nestorianism; he was rehabilitated by the Council of Chalcedon, which adopted in part his formulations of the christological dogma; under pressure from the emperor he was again finally condemned by Pope Vigilius and by the Second Council of Constantinople (553). In our time a careful doctoral thesis from the Gregorian concludes that Theodore's teaching "is substantially identical with the doctrine of that letter of Nestorius which was condemned at Ephesus,"[52] while a professor of the same Gregorian, one of the best scholars of early Church Christology, gives an affirmative answer to the question "whether, without expressing himself in the manner of St. Cyril of Alexandria, he would not however, as Cyril did, have recognized the Son of God in the son of the Virgin."[53]

Theodore's **Instructions for Catechumens** were also recently rediscovered.[54] But in contrast to Chrysos-

tom, Theodore does not avoid the christological problem. He dedicates several homilies to it. In order
to arm his catechumens against the Arian arguments,
he continually drills into them the distinction of the
two natures (e.g. **Hom.** 3, 6; 6, 3; 8, 10). Theodore is
the first author who uses this expression as a
regularly recurring technical term. Sometimes he
employs neuter forms such as "divinity" and "humanity," as Chrysostom does (e.g. **Hom.** 3, 4), but more
often he uses concrete expressions, as Diodore had
done:

> He was not only God, nor also only man,
> but he is by nature actually in both, God as
> well as man. He is God-Word, he who
> assumed, and he is the man who was assumed.
> And he who was God's form assumed the form
> of a slave; and the form of the slave is not
> the form of God. In the form of God he is the
> one who is by nature God, but the form of the
> slave is he who by nature is man, who was
> assumed for our salvation. He who assumed
> was thus not himself the one who was assumed;
> and he who was assumed was thus not the
> one who assumed; but he who assumed is God,
> while he who was assumed is man (**Hom.** 8, 1;
> cf. 6, 5).

And now something about the unity of both. For
Theodore, the man Jesus is no "ordinary man" (**Hom.**
5, 7; 6, 3) but still a true man born of Mary and

of our race (**Hom.** 6, 10), composed of body and soul, in which it would be wrong to exclude the **nous,** which indeed is the place of freedom and thus also of sin (**Hom.** 5, 9-17). This man fulfilled the natural law and the Mosaic law, and after his baptism became the model of evangelical life (**Hom.** 6, 2; 6, 8, 10-11; fr. **De Incarn.** XIII, **PG** 66, 988C; VII, col. 177C). But "God's grace guaranteed the man, who was assumed by God, against sin" (**Hom.** 5, 17). Because he was without sin, when he died in fulfillment of the law of death for mankind, he was raised up and glorified by God:

> Everything which belongs to human nature, he took for himself; after he was tested in all his capabilities, He perfected him through his power. Even when, according to the law of his nature, he underwent death, He did not separate himself from him . . . , but through the working of his grace, He freed him from death . . . , made him immortal, imperishable and unchangeable, and caused him to rise up to heaven. . . . There he now receives adoration on the grounds of his most intimate union with God the Word (**Hom.** 5, 5-6; 5, 18; 7, 13).

Thus the man Jesus, through his re-creation in resurrection and glorification, is the firstborn of the new mankind and of the new creation, who gives to everyone a share of his own fullness (**Hom.** 3, 9; 5, 21; 7, 9).

Theodore is the first writer in centuries who so clearly portrays Jesus' earthly life as the example and primary image of every Christian life with its struggle and its heavenly crowning. The Alexandrians were tempted to place the decisive moment of Jesus' divinization in his very incarnation and thus to regard the weakness of his earthly existence only as a veiling of his glory, which he already possessed even in his humanity. For Theodore, the glorification lies in the resurrection and ascension. This alone was bound to provoke opposition from the Alexandrian school. More dangerous, however, was Theodore's suggestion that Jesus first acquired sinlessness only through the resurrection: for this is the significance of the "unchangeableness of soul" (**Hom.** 5, 6; 6, 12), which we hear mentioned among the fruits of the resurrection. It is not as though he means that Jesus ever sinned; but Jesus' soul was also subject to this changeableness on earth and thus to the possibility of turning from God by which men come to sin. Only by grace and the uninterrupted nearness of the Word was he guaranteed against this possibility. From the other side, moreover, Theodore seems to see Jesus' sinlessness also as the guarantee of this nearness of the Word. There is also some truth in the statement that the human choice of Jesus is an element in the hypostatic union. That this union and this choice mutually condition one another, likewise seems to be admissible on condition that one possesses a sufficiently deep insight into the relationship between grace and freedom to realize that this mutual conditioning still remains permeated by the primacy of God's self-giving in grace and incarnation. During precisely this same period Augustine is wrestling with this very insight; Augustine likewise sees in Jesus' state of grace the primal image of every state of grace. Theodore seems also to have found this. But this was certainly not common opinion in the Greek church. Thus it was inevitable that, correctly or incorrectly, Theodore would be suspected of regarding the union of Jesus' humanity with the Word as a purely moral one.

This suspicion was further reinforced by Theodore's description of this union. Quite regularly he describes it as "adoption" or as "indwelling." But not infrequently he also uses the expression "one person" (**prosôpon**), which will become one of the pillars of the orthodoxy of Chalcedon. What does the term mean for Theodore? At Chalcedon the phrase "one person and one hypostasis" will be formulated, and this addition of "one hypostasis" will determine the meaning of "person." Indeed the word "person," which originally meant a mask and a dramatic role, can connote an element of fiction in which various individuals are regarded as one (think of our expres-

sion "a legal person"). Christians regularly used the
term to say that someone appeared in the name of
someone else (which means that they are validly
considered by the observer as one "person"); sometimes a prophet speaks in the "person" of the Father,
sometimes in that of the Son, and so on. In the
fourth century the word was introduced into the
doctrine of the Trinity. At first many regarded it
with suspicion, as if the "persons" of the Father and
the Son would be only different roles and forms of
appearance of the one God. In time the word
managed to be accepted and so Theodore, in addition
to speaking of three hypostases (independence) can
also speak of three "persons" (**Hom.** 3, 2-3). But to
what degree has this use of the word "person" as
signifying a "reality" penetrated Theodore's discussion of the incarnation? Does something of its old
significance still remain so that the Word and the
man Jesus are only regarded as one? At one time
he does set in contrast to the distinction of natures,
"the union in the person" (fr. **De Incarn.** XII, **PG** 66,
985B), but aside from this one instance, which was
translated by a later defender of Theodore, he never
says that the God-man would be "one and the same
through the union in the person" (**PG** 66, 970AB).
Rather, the term "one person" normally appears in
expressions such as: the Scripture "says both things
of the one person of the Son" (**Hom.** 3, 6-7; 6, 3;

8, 10-12), or "the man united with God receives this eminent honor through the union of the person" (**In. Ps.** 8, 1, ed. Devreesse, p. 43). Thus the term is used in a context in which the older meaning of "being-regarded-as" is still easily understood. Thus the expression "one person" cannot be of much further help in reconstructing Theodore's vision.

At first sight it may seem as though Theodore's analysis of the union between the Word which indwells and the man who is filled by him, clearly points in the direction of two persons. He argues namely that it is not through his "substance" or through his "operation" that God indwells in a special manner (**PG** 66, 972B). For according to his substance and his operation, God is present everywhere. Every special presence of God thus consists in a special "good pleasure" through which he is far from sinners but near to the just (973BC). God's special presence is never natural because his nature is omnipresent; rather it rests on a disposition of will (975CD).[55] Thus the special indwelling in the man Jesus also rests on God's special good pleasure, on grace.

Theodore poses for himself the problem that the indwelling which is the incarnation would be of the same order as the indwelling in the just. And to this he responds in the negative. In the first place, the man Jesus is filled with God from the very beginning, from the moment when he was formed in his mother's womb (976D, 977B, 994C; 997B). Consequently this union is indissoluble because the Word which dwelled in him gave to the man Jesus the power to bring all the good to fulfillment through his own freedom (976D; after the resurrection the union became more intimate; **ibid.**) and through his support he "guaranteed [him] unchangeable for all change toward evil" (977B; 989 Db). And above all this indwelling is unique, because it is an indwelling

> as in a son. For it is thus that he indwelled through good pleasure. But what does that mean: as in a son? That he so indwelled, that he completely united with himself him who was assumed; and that he granted to him to be participant in all the honor which the Son shares by nature; so that he perfected him to one person out of the power of the union with himself and shared with him all dominion (976BC).

Theodore therefore condemns Paul of Samosata (998A) and wants to hear nothing of a man who only after a period of time would be united with the Son of God: the union occurs at his conception in Mary's womb. And in this union Jesus' human freedom does form an essential element; but this freedom is given on credit within the eminent and indissoluble self-sharing of the Son. This self-sharing is grace, thus not natural or of natural necessity; but it assumes the man in the Sonship of the only Son, in his glory and dominion. Therefore Theodore can protest in all sincerity that he does not hold two sons or two Lords, although the Word is Son by nature and as primary symbol, but man by grace and secondarily (184D-985C: **prôtotupôs-hepomenôs**; cf. 1004A; 1017Cff.; **Hom. Cat.** 8, 10. 14). The Sonship of the man Jesus is indeed nothing other than the **grace**fully shared **natural** sonship.

> The union of the natures according to good pleasure brings it about that on the ground of their community of name the claim of both is one, the will, the operation, the authority, the might, the dominion, the value, the power; and in no way separated. So that from the strength of this union the persons of both sorts are and are called one. . . .

> Union according to substance can only exist between those who are one of substance; not between those who are of differing substances, because the union results in a confusion. But the union according to good pleasure preserves the natures without confusion and without division, and brings it about that the persons of both sorts are one, the will of both sorts and the operation of both sorts. . . .

> For, united with the Word, according to the manner of good pleasure, from the mother's

> womb, he remained indivisibly united because
> he had in all the same will and the same oper-
> ation. A more intimate union does not exist"
> (1012C-1013A).

This is a capable christological synthesis which gives evidence of vision and daring and likewise of deep respect for all the data of revelation. It contains elements of which Chalcedon will make grateful use, and which are still deserving of new consideration and reflection. It was Theodore's unmistakable intention to make the union as intimate and as all-embracing as it was possible for him to do. His sincere Catholic persuasion can hardly be called into question: this vehement knocking on the door witnesses to that. But at some point the door remains closed; a certain boundary still remains. Theodore will never say that the Son of God is "one and the same" with the man Jesus, that he himself is this man. After having, in opposition to the Arians, once distinguished the divine and the human in the Lord as "one and another" (only Chrysostom discarded this formula), the Antiochene school seems predisposed to halt before this boundary. And yet is it not precisely there that the heart of the good news lies, that the Father has sent his eternal Son himself on earth, that this Son himself has experienced our existence, that this Son himself was handed over to death for us sinners and raised up for our justification? It is precisely Theodore's **Catecheses**, so rich in other respects, which show how this preoccupation with making a pure distinction between the human and the divine hampers the power of his message (and moreover distorts his doctrine of the Trinity).

It has been said, both recently and in the past, that Chalcedon actually did nothing other than canonize Theodore's Christology. There are indeed many elements of Chalcedon's definition to be found in the Antiochene teacher: "two natures," "one person," "without confusion and without division." But the definition adds one element which is not found in Theodore: "the **same** perfect in his divinity and the **same** perfect in his humanity." And this element is everything. Before the usable building blocks of Theodore's Christology could be taken up in the canonical teaching of the Church, this fundamental insight had to be securely established. It remains for us to treat of the manner, dramatic and tragic in its consequences, in which this came about through the Council of Ephesus.

c. Nestorius and Cyril: The Council of Ephesus (431)

The frontal confrontation between this renewed form of the Antiochene theology and the Christology of Alexandria was so explosive that the Church was rocked on her foundations and the tremors continued to be felt for centuries.

Several factors contributed to this violence. First there was the fact that the rivalry between the old patriarchates was soured by the arrival of the **parvenu** Constantinople which, thanks to the imperial court, threatened to outflank both, and by the memory of the drama in which Cyril's uncle and predecessor had so bitterly played a part in the downfall of the other Antiochene on the seat of Constantinople, Chrysostom. Further there was the fact that this was not only a clash of personal convictions, but that behind each of the champions stood a school possessing a worthy tradition of at least a century. And the intellectual character and personality of both men made its own contribution: Nestorius, a second-rate theologian who with learned obstinancy and sharp dialectic held fast to the teaching of his master without sharing in his evangelical inspiration; Cyril, whose holy indignation easily degenerated into an iron determination to destroy his opponent and then shrank from no means to achieve this. Moreover, it seems that the two antagonists so little comprehended the existence of a school other than their own that they were completely surprised and bewildered by the teaching of the other; each was so confident of the strength of his position that he hurled himself recklessly into the struggle.

But behind and beneath all these factors lies a genuine clash of convictions: their fundamental conception of the person and of the work of Christ is different and we can easily recognize here the very disagreement of the propositions of the New Testament Christology. For the Alexandrians, Christ is the eternal Word, who now clothes himself with human form and thus appears among us. The deepest core of the human existence of Jesus is the very existence of the eternal Son. It is thus a glorified and deified existence. For the Antiochenes, on the other hand, Jesus is a man, so intimately and all-embracingly united with the Word of the Father that in perfect trust he follows God unto death and is therefore glorified: this man is taken up in the Sonship of the eternal Son.

For the Alexandrians this union is a **phusice,** which is given with the very existence of this human nature (**phusis**); it is thus perfect from the very moment of the incarnation; the sanctity of this man is a substantial one, which expresses itself in his deeds, but is not first realized through these deeds; Jesus' humanity is from the first moment deified and glorified, and only for a time veiled through the weakness of his

earthly solidarity with the rest of the children of
Adam.

The theologians of Antioch, on the other hand,
emphasize that this union is the work of God's free
grace: it is a wonder and has nothing of the necessity
of nature; and from the side of the man assumed
this union includes a humanly free (although not
fallible) agreement; so this union can grow with the
very growth of Jesus' human consciousness; his
sanctity was certainly granted in principle in the
initial union, but was realized through the human
deeds of the Lord; thus his perfect glorification and
deification is also the reward for his human holiness,
and is given him in resurrection and ascension.

Ever since Athanasius, the Alexandrians have regarded the decisive moment of the redemption as
being especially the moment of the incarnation itself.
The men of Antioch regard this moment as being that
of cross and resurrection.

Thus at the basis of this conflict lies the fact that
the Alexandrians work from the supposition that the
eternal Son himself is also the subject of Jesus' human
existence: he is one divine Someone, who, remaining
what he is, has become man. The Antiochenes are
preoccupied with the fear that in this way the genuine

divinity of the Son is violated: thus they continue to speak of "one and another" even as they recognize that the eternal Son of God and the Son of Mary form the one Christ.

The occasion for the explosive clash is the term "Mother of God," **theotokos.** This title was in current use certainly from the beginning of the fourth century even in circles outside the properly Alexandrian school: Eustathius of Antioch had used the word;[16] and Gregory of Nazianzus, in his great christological letter, had even pronounced an anathema over those who did not wish to see in Mary the Mother of God (**Ep.** 101, **PG** 37, 177C). But Diodore and Theodore manifested opposition against this title, which they were reluctant to accept without qualification (Theodorus Mops. fr. **PG** 66, 992f.)[17] It is characteristic of Nestorius' character that he did not hesitate to make a frontal attack on this title.

From the moment that the Antiochene monk and preacher, Nestorius, was raised by the emperor to be Patriarch of Constantinople (428), he dedicated himself to the task of exterminating all the errors in his diocesan city: five days after his enthronement the police closed the chapel of the Arians, and within several weeks an imperial law appeared which banished a motley line of heretical groups from the city (**Cod. Theod.** XVI, V, 65). His struggle against the title **theotokos** also apparently belongs in this great move toward purification. In Nestorius' presence, Dorotheus of Marcianapolis stated in a sermon: "Anathema if anyone names Mary the Mother of God" (Cyrillus, **Ep.** 8, **PG** 77, 60B). This caused understandable commotion among the faithful of Constantinople and especially among the numerous monks of the imperial city. In a series of sermons Nestorius argues that Mary is Mother of the man and Mother of Christ, but not Mother of God:

> Everywhere (in Scripture) it is preached that the Virgin is the mother of the child, not of the divinity. . . . It is a great thing that the Christ-bearing mother bears a humanity which is the instrument of the divinity of the God-Word, . . . that she bears a Mediator who is united with the dignity of God (**Fragm. Serm.** VIII, ed. Loofs, **Nestoriana,** p. 247).

> The divinity is "without mother" and Mary has borne not the divinity "but a man, organ of the divinity and its temple" (**ibid.,** IX, p. 252).

Nestorius later explained what he objected to in this title: Arianism and Apollinarianism (**ibid.** X, pp. 272f.). He fears that the use of this title strengthens the theory that the Son of God had a temporal beginning.

The events quickly follow one another. Cyril of

Alexandria becomes alarmed. He writes to Nestorius
in a relatively benevolent tone, scarcely able to be-
lieve that the rumors are true; but if Nestorius has
said something in the heat of discourse, let him then
set matters right by naming Mary the Mother of God
(**Ep.** 2, **PG** 77, 41c).

But Cyril has already sent a christological treatise
to the monks of Constantinople which acts as oil on
the fire of their resistance. Nestorius responds coolly.
A second letter of Cyril's presents a commentary on
the definition of Nicaea and warns him to think
accordingly; this letter will later be endorsed by the
Council of Ephesus (**Ep.** 4, col. 44-49). Nestorius'
reply is extremely haughty: Cyril has not understood
anything of Nicaea, an insulting accusation for the
man who calls himself the successor of Athanasius;
this letter will be condemned at Ephesus (**Ep.** 5, col.
49-52). Both parties forward these letters to Pope
Celestine in Rome. The accompanying writings of
Nestorius display a characteristic lack of tact. Cyril's
writing, on the other hand, is a masterpiece exhibiting
a holy perturbation that is concerned with the situation in Constantinople and a humble desire to accept
the decision of Rome; the body of the letter touches
only on the **theotokos** question, but an appendix portrays Nestorius as a reincarnation of Paul of Samosata
(**Ep.** 11, col. 80-85). Pope Celestine summons a Synod

which condemns the teaching of Nestorius; in a letter
of August 11, 430, he appoints Cyril as his proxy:
he is to summon Nestorius to repent of his errors and,
in case he refuses, Cyril is to excommunicate him
(**Ep.** 12, col. 89-93). The other patriarchs were also
informed of this decision. In the autumn of the same
year Cyril also holds a Synod in Alexandria: in a
lengthy letter, Cyril sets out the true doctrine for
the sake of Nestorius and he appends to this twelve
anathemas (**DS** 252-263), which Nestorius will have to
sign (**Ep.** 17, col. 105-122). In this weighty piece Cyril
makes a fatal mistake. In searching for a description
of the unity which will allow for no loopholes, he
thinks he has discovered the right formula in the
expression "natural union" (**henôsis physikê:** Anathema
2) which he believes to have been formulated by
Athanasius; actually it stems, rather, from Apollinaris, some of whose writings were collected under
the name of Athanasius. For Nestorius and the
Antiochenes, this strengthened the impression that
Apollinarianism was alive again in Cyril.

Finally Nestorius realized the seriousness of the
situation. He requested the emperor Theodosius to
summon an ecumenical council: the Council of
Ephesus. By the middle of June, 431, Cyril and
Nestorius and approximately two hundred bishops
had arrived in Ephesus, but John of Antioch was

still on the way with his suffragans, just as were the legates of the Pope. But the date set for the opening of the Council had already come and gone; and Cyril forced the opening. In spite of the protest of the imperial commissioner and of sixty bishops, he held the first session on June 22, with about one hundred and fifty bishops. On that same day a decision was reached. On three occasions Nestorius was called to appear before the Council. He refused. Then the definition of Nicaea was read aloud as the established norm of the faith; then the second letters of both Cyril and Nestorius were read to the assembly. The former was unanimously approved as being in agreement with Nicaea; that of Nestorius, on the other hand, was condemned as being in opposition to that Council. Still on the same day came the decree for the condemnation and dismissal of Nestorius. The essential dogmatic task of the Council of Ephesus, about which we shall have more to say, was completed.

Two days later John of Antioch arrived. He also lost no time: in a gathering of sixty bishops, Cyril was condemned because of his uncanonical procedures and because of the Arian and Apollinarian errors in his anathemas (June 26). Finally, at the beginning of July, the Roman legates also arrived; in accordance with their instructions they joined sides with Cyril. They had the minutes of the June 22 session read for them and ratified the condemnation of Nestorius; subsequently John of Antioch and his supporters were excommunicated by Cyril and his Council.

The confusion was absolute. Emperor Theodosius felt he could save the situation by a Solomonlike judgment: he ratified the condemnation of Nestorius as well as that of Cyril and had both arrested. Further he disbanded the Council. After several months he allowed Cyril to return to Alexandria, while Nestorius was sent back to his former cloister in Antioch and a successor replaced him in Constantinople. The tragic ending of the Council of Ephesus was that Cyril (along with Rome) and John of Antioch had excommunicated each other. This situation necessitated wearying exchanges and dogmatic discussions which after several years finally led to a favorable outcome.

The Council of Ephesus promulgated no real confession of faith, but it did condemn Nestorius' christological theory as being in conflict with Nicaea and approved the second letter of Cyril (his third letter containing the anathemas was added only in the Acts). Thus these two letters are of eminent importance for the development of Christology.

In his above-mentioned letter to Cyril, Nestorius claims that the Alexandrian's explanation of the definition of Nicaea makes the Word passible because it allows the divine Person himself to be born from the Virgin and permits him to suffer and to die. According to Nestorius, both Scripture and Nicaea have already attributed this saving event to Christ, that is to say:

> to this name, which signifies the passible as well as the impassible substance in one person (**prosôpon**): so that Christ can be called passible and impassible without danger, impassible according to his divinity, passible according to the nature of his flesh (**PG** 77, 52BC).

To be precise, Mary must be called the Mother of Christ, not the Mother of God (53B), for to state that the Word is born of the Virgin is either paganism or the heresy of Arius and Apollinaris (53B, 56A). From Mary is born the temple who, from his mother's womb, is so intimately united with the Word that the fate of this temple is appropriated by the Word (56A).

Nestorius thus clearly rejects the adoptionism of Paul of Samosata, according to whom Jesus was first an ordinary man who then later became united with the Son of God. For Nestorius, this union occurs from the mother's womb and thus includes the entire human existence of Jesus. But he refuses to

accept any temporal attributes of the Word: these
can only come to the Son of God insofar as he has
assumed the man and thus insofar as he is referred
to by names which express this twofoldness of natures,
names such as Christ, Lord, Son (because in imitation
of Nicaea he definitely wants to adhere to the teaching about "one Son and Lord," Nestorius must argue
that "Son" is not a title of the divine Person as such
but only of the incarnate: 52AB). Supposedly, Nestorius intends to do nothing else than to assert that
the temporal saving deeds may not be attributed to
the divine nature itself of the Son of God. In this
he is completely orthodox. But he draws from this
the conclusion that these temporal saving acts may
not be attributed to the divine subject as such, but
only to the composite subject which is Christ, the
eternal Son plus the assumed man. Even this can
still have an orthodox meaning when "divine Subject
as such" is understood to signify "the divine subject
in virtue of his divine nature." Supposedly this is all
that Nestorius means to say; but in fact he says more
and refuses to call the divine Person himself the
ultimate subject of the mysteries of salvation.

Undoubtedly the Council does not condemn the
details of Nestorius' terminology: two natures or
substances (**ousia**), one person—for this, more fundamental discussion was needed—but his refusal to say

that the one divine Person himself is the subject of the events of salvation.

That is precisely what Cyril placed foremost in the letter which was endorsed by the Council: "The only begotten Son himself, who according to his nature was born of God the Father . . . came down, became flesh and man, has suffered, rose on the third day, and ascended into heaven" (45C).

Likewise Cyril understands that "the divine nature of the Word is not altered by changing . . . into a man, who is composed of soul and body," and "that the natures which are united in genuine unity are different" (45BC), that thus "his divine nature did not begin to exist in the holy Virgin" (45C; 48D). Incarnation means for him "that the Word united himself in a substantial manner (**kath'hypostasin**) with the flesh which is animated by a rational soul, . . . and not only by will or good pleasure, or only by the assumption of a **prosôpon** (45B)," through which he would only function as man without actually being so.

The Son of God makes the flesh his own and thus genuinely appropriates the birth from the Virgin, the suffering, the death, and the resurrection. Not as if his divine nature had undergone all this—that would be absurd—but owing to the fact that he makes the animated flesh his own, it is he himself who in the flesh is born from Mary, who died and rose (48AB). Whoever rejects this substantial union, that is to say, whoever denies that the Son of God and the Son of man are one "thing" (**hypostasis=pragma: Apologet c. Theod., PG** 76, 396C) also must necessarily distinguish two sons, despite the fact that he accepts "one union of persons" through which both function as one (48BC).

In this letter Cyril does not use the expressions "one nature" and "natural union," which appear in his **Anathemas** and which will give rise to so much exasperation and resistance. He recognizes that the distinction of natures remains. But the union of the two is not accidental; it is not only a union through good pleasure or in **prosôpon** but is substantial and thus determines the deepest being of this man and effects that the Son of God himself is the subject of the human existence of Jesus. "Two natures," union "according to hypostase": these will become the key terms of the definition of Chalcedon. Because the Council of Ephesus canonizes this letter of Cyril, the way is open for these terms. But even here, Ephesus does not intend to enter into the worthiness of Cyril's terminology; the Council makes the general intent of the letter its own: the eternal Son of the Father is himself the one who is born from Mary, dies, and rises. He is the one subject· of the saving mystery. Without becoming involved in terminological questions, Ephesus defines that Jesús of Nazareth is the eternal Son himself of the Father, and thus affirms the true union of the God-man.

The tragedy of this Council was that at the same time the genuine and complete humanity of Jesus again appeared to be being violated, and this precisely by the dominant figure of the Council, Cyril of Jerusalem. The completeness of the humanity could not be excluded, or the definition of the unity would be seriously compromised.

4. From Ephesus to Chalcedon

a. Cyril's Development

Ephesus ended in the mutual excommunication of two great patriarchs of the East, John of Antioch and Cyril of Alexandria. And yet the difference in doctrine between the two was less serious than was able to be perceived. In contrast to the great Council, the Synod of John and the Eastern bishops did issue a Christological confession of faith:

> We confess our Lord Jesus Christ, only begotten Son of God, fully God and fully man of a rational soul and a body; before the ages born of the father according to the divinity, and **the same** in the end of days . . . born of

Mary according to the humanity; **the same** of
one nature (**homoousios**) with the Father
according to the divinity, and of one nature
with us according to humanity. A unity came
to exist between the natures and therefore we
can confess one Christ, one Lord, one Son.
By reason of this union without confusion we
confess that the holy Virgin is the Mother of
God, because the God-Word became flesh and
in the incarnation and from the conception on
has united with himself the temple which he
has taken on from her (**Mansi** V. 783CD).

This confession of faith was not probably drawn
up by Theodoret of Cyrrhus (d. **ca.** 457-466), a disciple
of Theodore of Mopsuestia. But by naming Mary the
Mother of God without reservation, and by expressly
affirming the identity of the Son of God and the Son
of man, these Antiochene bishops show that they
have freed themselves from the limitations of the
Antiochene school, which in Nestorius had become
as rigid as stone. Characteristic for the Antiochene
approach remains the symmetrical structure of the
Christ-image out of two natures. Cyril's approach
remains more concentric: the Word who clothes
himself with animated flesh and thus is also the
deepest center of the Lord's human life.[58] But, for
the rest, there are scarcely any differences of importance between the Antiochene confession and
the Christology of Cyril's second letter.

And yet it was the intention of John and Theodoret to mark Cyril as a heretic by means of this confession of faith. By naming the God-man "fully man" and "of one nature with us," they aim at condemning the Apollinarianism which they think they recognize in Cyril's **Anathemas.** This was a misunderstanding, but one which is quite understandable. Cyril was certainly no Apollinarian; he continually emphasized, for example in his second letter to Nestorius, that the flesh of the Lord was animated by a rational soul, and he spoke of two natures. But the **Anathemas** used Apollinarian terms: "one nature" and "natural union," and thus gave the impression that because of the union the "flesh" of the Lord was of a different and more divine nature than our own. Cyril used "nature" in varying meanings. For all of his contemporaries, this word signified not the abstract "nature," the "essence," but a "reality of a particular kind."[59] Sometimes "a reality" was emphasized, and then for Cyril the God-man is "one nature," one Something, one living being. Sometimes the emphasis rested on "of a particular kind," and then Cyril can distinguish the divine and the human as different natures. The Antiochenes were familiar only with this latter usage and detected Apollinarianism in the first: a fusion of the divine and human into one new sort of being. The following years were filled with lively and passionate discussions which for the most part dealt with terminology and with which we shall not concern ourselves.[60] It is of more importance for our purpose that, although Cyril never overcame his ambiguous usage of this term, these discussions resulted in an essential enrichment of his christological insight.

After wearisome attempts toward mediation, communication between Cyril and John was re-established in 433 on the basis of a christological formula, the Symbol of Union, which was nothing other than Theodoret's confession of faith quoted above. John acknowledges the condemnation of Nestorius and quietly drops his attack on the **Anathemas.** Cyril enthusiastically accepts the Symbol of Union as a restatement of the faith of Nicaea and does not demand acceptance of his **Anathemas.** Nonetheless, as has already been said, alongside the two-natures formula he will continue to use the formula of "the one incarnate nature of the God-Word," partially out of fidelity toward its supposed author, Athanasius. From now on he will have to fight with an uncertain terminology on two fronts: against the Antiochenes who continue to reproach his "Apollinarianism," and against the Cyrilians, who see in the acceptance of the Symbol of Union a betrayal of the **Anathemas.** The extremists of the first group continue to reject the Council of Ephesus and will be known as Nestorians; those of the second group will reject Chalcedon in the name of the **Anathemas** and go through history known as the Monophysites. Whether either "heresy" is more than a question of semantics and stubbornness remains doubtful till the present day.

Just how thorny Cyril's position was, but likewise just how stimulating for his thought, can be seen, for example, from his letters to Succensus in which he argues that the one-nature formula is in perfect harmony with the Symbol of Union (**PG** 77, 228-245). In these letters he unconditionally recognizes that the incarnation may not entail any change of the human into the divine nature, thus no violation of the **homoousia** of the God-man with us (241D), and likewise no assumption of the function of the human soul by the Word (240BC). Here he employs expressions which will later be adopted in Chalcedon: "The two natures are joined together in an indissoluble union without confusion and without change" (232BC) so that "each of the two remains in its natural character" (241B).

This insight into the permanent character of the human leads Cyril to introduce nuances into the principle of the "deification through assumption" and thus to take an essential step in Christology (233B-236D).

There are various indications of this development

in Cyril. As we have seen above, the emphasis in
the redemption doctrine as it was worked out by
Athanasius and in the polemic against Apollinarianism
lay on the moment of the incarnation; there it was
that the new, deified man was raised up who, as
firstborn, is the source for all. In this same sense
Cyril's eleventh Anathema spoke of the "life-giving
flesh" of the Lord (**DS** 262). But in the · letter to
Succensus he says that this flesh becomes divinized
and life-giving through the resurrection (**PG** 77, 236B).
Here then is a new appreciation of Jesus' earthly life
and activity which is the way from the initial and
fundamental union with the Son of God toward a
full-grown divinization. Another evidence is that
Cyril revises the common conception of Christ's
priesthood; (moreover his contemporary, Augustine,
did the same thing in the West). The sacrifice of
the Lord was customarilly described by saying that
the Word was the high priest and that his "flesh,"
that is, his humanity, was the passive victim. It
was nowhere claimed that the man also offered himself. Thanks to his intense reflection on Scripture
(it is remarkable how often the Epistle to the
Hebrews is cited in his writing after Ephesus), Cyril
rediscovers the insight that the God-man does not
have a formal priestly function according to his divinity but, rather, in power of his incarnation. He "became our high priest, who as man performs the

liturgical service by offering his own body to the
Father" (**Ad Reginas** II. 43, **PG** 76, 1396B), and he
"mediates as man, . . . and is himself the victim and
himself the priest" (**In Joh.** XI. 8, **PG** 74, 505Db).

Then it is rather self-evident that this human
sacrifice of self must also be truly an act of perfect
human freedom and love; Jesus' sacrifice must be
"rational and voluntary" even according to his humanity (**Ep. ad Succ.** II, **PG** 77, 244D).[61]

While Apollinaris had made the union of will and
the related sanctity into a fundamental principle of
his system, and while the Antiochenes spoke of the
one will of Christ, Cyril recognized a real distinction
between his divine and his human will, between
which there can even be a certain tension.   The
divine willing is the will of God who he himself **is** as
Word (**In Joh.** X. 15, 9, **PG** 74, 373B); the human
willing is the expression of his genuine human nature
(**In Luc.** 22, 29, **PG** 72, 921D).

In this following text especially, a commentary on
the story of Gethsemane, the meaning of Cyril's teaching becomes clear. The Son of God has taken on not
only a static human nature, but a human life, and
that a life in the family of Adam. By this he has
subjected himself to the law of death, and to the
law by which man recoils from death. There is in

man, and also in this Man, a natural resistance against
the law of death which God had decreed for the
family of man. But because this man is permeated
by the Son of God himself, he conquers this natural
resistance in perfect filial obedience. Thus, by his
obedient death, Jesus conquers the kingdom of disobedience and of death; thus he is raised up and his
"flesh" becomes a source of life for his brothers.

> Likewise in Christ the human is moved
> in two ways . . . (in the first place by fear and
> anxiety, which are natural human movements
> of the soul). From the other side . . . in order
> to be overcome by the power of the Word
> so that in Christ as the firstling the nature (of
> man) would be recreated to a better and more
> divine state. For that was the only way in
> which the healing could also penetrate into us.
> For although everything that happened was
> not in every respect desired by him, for the
> sake of the redemption and the life of all, he
> made the suffering of the cross something
> voluntary. . . . The Word of God indeed be-
> came man for no other reason than to unite
> his (nature) with our weaknesses, and by this
> to strengthen the nature of man and to change
> it into his own firmness. . . . For also in Christ
> himself the nature of man, considered in itself,
> is weak, but through the Word which is united
> with it, it is elevated to divine firmness" (**In
> Luc.** 22/39, **PG** 72, 921D-924C; cf. **Scholia de**

Incarn. 8, **PG** 75, 1377B; **Ad Reginas** II. 43, **PG** 76, 1396B).

More than any of his predecessors since Irenaeus, Cyril has seriously dealt with the teaching that the Son of God became man in the family of Adam. He is completely and fully man even including the weaknesses—sin excepted—of his brothers of the race of Adam.

But by the fact that he, from the power of the Son he is, lives through and suffers through these weaknesses in genuinely human but sinless obedience, he gives to the weak children of Adam the power to become children of God. For Cyril the old exchange principle not only states: Through the fact that the Son becomes man, men become sons, but also: Through the fact that the Son led a human life on the old earth, he enables us to live as sons and thus to attain the new earth. The incarnation of God signifies no curtailment of his genuine human life, for "through the union . . . (the God-Word) preserved the humanity in what it was . . ., but fulfilled it also with the operation of his power" (**Scholia de Incarn.** 9, **PG** 75, 1380B).

b. The Council of Chalcedon (451)

Cyril's disciples did not possess his deep insight,

which was able to recognize the elements of truth present in other schools of thought. They bound themselves fast to the letter of his **Anathemas**. Four years after Cyril's death, Eutyches, the leader of the monks of Constantinople, opened an attack on the suspected Nestorianism of some bishops. But at the Synod of Constantinople (448) he was himself condemned by Bishop Flavian because, in rigidly clinging to the formula of the one-nature, Eutyches refused to recognize that the incarnate Son is out of two natures and that according to his human nature he is "of one nature" with us (**Mansi** VI. 741-744). The most that he was willing to concede was "that our Lord is of two natures before the union, but after the union I confess one nature" (744AB).

Flavian of Constantinople, on the contrary, recognized that with Cyril one can speak of the "one incarnate nature of the God-Word," but at the same time he maintained "that after becoming flesh and man Christ is out of two natures, in one hypostasis and in one person (**prosôpon**), one Christ, one Son, one Lord" (**Mansi** VI. 541AC; **ACO** II. 1, 1, p. 35). Pope Leo the Great ratified the condemnation of Eutyches, and clarified the doctrine about Christ in a very lengthy letter to Flavian, the **Tomus ad Flavianum** (early in 449):

The same eternal Son of the eternal Father

was born out of the Holy Spirit and the Virgin
Mary. This birth in time has done no damage
to his eternal birth . . . , but is wholly directed
to re-establish man who was lost. . . . For we
would not be able to conquer the prince of
sin and death if he had not taken on our
nature and made it his own, who could not be
defiled by sin nor dominated by death . . .
(**Mansi** V. 1368CD).

With the preservation thus of the property
of each nature and substance, and because
they joined together in one person, the divinity
took on our littleness, the power our weakness,
the immortal our mortality. And in order to
liquidate the debt of our state, the inviolable
nature had united itself with the mortal nature,
. . . so that one and the same, the mediator of
God and men, the man Jesus Christ, from the
one side could die, and from the other not.
Thus the true God is born in a complete and
perfect human nature, complete in what is
proper to him, complete in what is proper to us.

What is proper to us, I say, namely what
the Creator has created in us from the beginning and what he came to restore. For what
the liar has introduced and what duped man
has admitted, has left no trace in the Savior.
And although he has shared in our weaknesses,
he did not participate in our misdeeds. . . .
Thus he who has made man in the image of
God, the same became man in the form of

a slave. For each nature preserves its property unviolated . . . (**Mansi** V. 1371D-1374C).

He who is true God, the same is true man. In this union nothing is deceitful because the littleness of man and the greatness of the divinity are each other. For God is not changed by this act of mercy, and the man not consumed by the (divine) worth. For, in community with the other, each form brings forth what is proper to it; the Word works what is proper to the Word, and the flesh accomplishes what is proper to the flesh. The one radiates in miracles, the other is silent under violence. . . . For—this must continually be repeated— one and the same is truly the Son of God and truly the Son of men . . . (1375-1378A). To make this unity of person in two natures known, it is written that the Son of man came down from heaven . . . , and that the Son of God was crucified and buried, although he did not suffer this in his divinity . . . , but in the weakness of his human nature" (1379CD).

The writings of Flavian and Leo were to become of decisive importance. The first introduced into Christology the pairing of the words **prosôpon** and **hypostasis,** which was already common practice in the doctrine of the Trinity. This removed the suspicion that the one **prosôpon** in Christ meant only that the God and the man in him simply function and are regarded as one: for the word "hypostasis," or substance, has a meaning burdened with reality: "it is the firm basis from out of which the existing, the standing, possesses itself and develops";[62] it signifies no one other than the very person of the eternal Son of God. And with Leo the full weight of the Latin christological thought was thrown into the scale, that thought which had arrived at a great maturity and firmness from Tertullian through the work of Hilary, Ambrose, Augustine, and through contact with Athanasius, the Cappadocians, and Cyril.

First the united forces of Constantinople and Rome suffered a crushing defeat. Eutyches was able to obtain from Emperor Theodosius II a hearing before a great Council in Ephesus. At this "Robber Synod" (449), the Patriarch of Alexandria, Cyril's successor Dioscorus, again was in charge. Supported by the military and by bands of monks this man managed to intimidate the bishops into declaring Eutyches to be orthodox and condemning and deposing Flavian. The latter died a short time later as the result of being mistreated. But Eutyches' imperial protector also died.

In consultation with Leo, the new emperor, Marcian, called a general Council in Chalcedon (451). With its nearly six hundred bishops, among whom were three papal legates and two representatives of Latin Africa, this became by far the largest Council

of early times. At the first sessions the legality of
the Robber Synod was examined in the light of the
Acts and of the testimony of numerous persons who
were present there. Dioscorus was condemned on
account of his violence, and the condemnation of
Eutyches by Flavian was ratified. The bishops were
not interested in a new confession of faith: the
definitions of Nicaea and Constantinople (381) along
with the clarification in Leo's **Tomus** were sufficient
(**Mansi** VI. 953AB). But the representatives of the
emperor continued to insist upon a definition of the
christological dogma. A commission of bishops then
worked out a schema; the text is not preserved, but
it appears that this schema declared that Christ is
"out of two natures" without making it clear whether
this meant that, after the incarnation, he also continues to exist "out of two natures" (this was the
opinion of Flavian) or that "out of two natures before
the incarnation" he became one nature (Eutyches'
position).

The majority of the bishops went along with this
ambiguous formula. But the papal legates forcefully
protested and even threatened to move the Council
to Italy. When they also gained support from the
imperial commissioners who backed this threat in
the name of the emperor and faced the bishops
squarely with the dilemma of choosing either for

Dioscorus or for Leo, the bishops finally conceded (**Mansi** VII. 104-105). A new commission, whose members now also included the Roman legates and the imperial commissioners, drew up a profession of faith which was accepted by the Council.

The definition of Chalcedon[63] contains, first of all, the profession of Nicaea and of the First Council of Constantinople (381); then it attaches its highest approval to Cyril's second letter to Nestorius and to his writings, along with the Symbol of Union of 433, "which are in agreement with each other" (**Mansi** VII. 113B), and also to the **Tomus** of Leo, which condemns those "who imagine that before the union there are two natures of the Lord, but that after the union make one (nature) of them" (116A). Finally the Council gives its own definition:

> 1. In imitation of the holy fathers we confess with one voice that our Lord Jesus Christ is one and the same Son . . . ; the same perfect in his divinity and the same perfect in his humanity;

> 2. truly God and the same truly man of a rational soul and a body;

> 3. of one nature with the Father according to the divinity, and the same of one nature with us according to the humanity, in all things like us except in sin;

4. before the ages begotten of the Father according to the divinity, but the same in the last days, for us and for our salvation, (born) according to the humanity of Mary the Virgin and Mother of God;

5. one and the same Christ, Lord, Only-begotten, in two natures;

6. without confusion, without change, without division, and without separation.

7. The difference of the natures is not removed through the union but, rather, the property of each nature is preserved and they coalesce in one person (**prosôpon**) and one independence (**hypostasis**);

9. not divided or separated into two persons,

10. but one and the same only-begotten Son, God-Word, Jesus-Christ the Lord (**DS** 301-302).

One can only contend that this definition was drawn up in connection with the **Tomus**[64] of Leo if he concentrates his attention exclusively on the formal schema of the one person in two natures. The influence of Cyril in his second letter to Nestorius and of the Symbol of Union is incomparably more significant.

The first section (1-4) was borrowed with editorial alterations from the Symbol of Union; but because the words "one and the same" have been added, especially in the position of emphasis at the opening of the text (which does not come out in the translation) this thesis of Cyril's gains an even stronger relief.

"In two natures" (5) is a formula of Leo's, which is an important improvement on the "out of two natures" of Flavian, which had become ambiguous in the mouth of Eutyches. "Without confusion" (6) we found already in Tertullian, and later in Chrysostom; in the meantime it had become common property; it is used to express that in the union, the divine and the human remain themselves actually and un-curtailed ("without change") and that the two natures do not flow into one another and result in something new which would be neither God nor man. Rather, the divine and the human are likewise bound "without division, and without separation" (6): they can be distinguished within the unity of "one and the same" but never separated. This complete four-part formula originated in the course of the debates of the Council, supposedly under the influence of the Roman legates (**ACO** II. 1, 2 p. 102/39; p. 125/18). That "the difference of the natures is not removed through the union" (7a) is a formula of Cyril's letter to Nestorius which states the same thing as "without confusion and without change"; that "the property of each nature is preserved" (7b) again repeats the same thing in words

which can be found in Cyril and Leo and also in
Tertullian. "One person" (8) is likewise a formula of
Tertullian which had long since become common
property in the West; in the Antiochene school it had
a dubious meaning and Cyril had rejected it as un-
satisfactory; but by the addition of "and one independence" Flavian had indicated that the word "person" here had the same reality-significance as in the
doctrine of the Trinity: it is actually the divine Person
of the eternal Son who lives and is in this human
nature, as is stressed in (10).

Thus this profession of Chalcedon forms a remarkable mosaic of stones gathered from various quarries:
the old Latin tradition is represented here, but also
Cyril and his opponent Theodoret, who indeed had
composed the Symbol of Union. What is truly
amazing is that in spite of all this, a powerful and
homogeneous text resulted in which the unique contribution of each of the schools was placed in service
of the communal believing insight. "One and the
same"—this ancient truth of the tradition forms the
basic pattern of this definition. And this is a definite
victory for the school of Alexandria: in the man
Jesus of Nazareth it is the Son of God himself who
appears and lives. Athanasius and Cyril have had to
fight with all their strength to preserve this basic
insight against the two-fold attack which was directed

against it: against the Arians who saw in the incarnation the proof that the Son is not truly God;
against the Nestorians who sacrificed the unity in
order to save the complete divinity. "Truly God"
and "of one nature with the Father": not an inferior
heavenly being come to save us and reconcile us
with the Father, but the substantially identical Son
himself, who is in the bosom of the Father. And yet
also "truly man of a rational soul and a body" and
"of one nature with us"; the Antiochene school has
fought for this against the old Docetism and also
against certain tendencies in Origenism. Jesus of
Nazareth was truly one of us and of our race, man
as we, but through his union with the Son more holy
than we, and the original source of our sanctification.
As Irenaeus had already supposed, the incarnation of
the Creator-Word cannot signify any curtailment or
mutilation of the humanity, but must accomplish
precisely the full and absolute realization of humanity. He is the perfect and complete man, because
he himself is the creator of man: because the divine
Idea of humanity itself becomes man, God raises up
the ideal Man. And in order to put this mystery of
God's grace and of the re-creation of man into words
—the sober framework of Tertullian's formula: one
person, in two natures. The Council makes no effort
to work out in more detail the meaning of these
terms, the general purport of which was sufficiently

familiar from the doctrine of the Trinity: the person
indicates **who** he is, namely the eternal Son of God
himself; the natures indicate **what** he is, substantially
one with the Father and also substantially one with
us. The Council correctly left any further determination of these concepts to the studies of Byzantine
and Latin Scholasticism.

There is however another lacuna in this definition,
which is in one sense disappointing. No mention is
made of the saving work of the Lord and of the
significance for salvation which his incarnation and
his human activities have for us. Cyril was dead, Leo
was far away, Theodoret of Cyrrhus sat at the Council
more or less as one accused. Among the leading
figures of Chalcedon there was apparently no one
who completely perceived what connection lay between the constitution of the God-man and his work
of salvation. A partial explanation for this lacuna
apparently lies in the formalistic cult of words and
concepts which was commonly characteristic for
epigonoi and which was brought to an extreme in
the debates about "person," "hypostasis," and "nature."
Perhaps a deeper explanation can be found in the
dominant position which Athanasius' version of the
exchange principle still possessed and according to
which the very being of the God-man is the definitive moment in the redemption: Cyril's disciples had

not yet made his later developments their own. And as an excusing factor, it must be further pointed out that this christological definition was only one section of a more inclusive profession of faith in which the first, and for the Council fathers principal, part is nothing other than the definitions of Nicaea and of Constantinople. These latter proclaimed that the only begotten Son of the Father became incarnate of Mary, suffered under Pontius Pilate, died, and on the third day rose. The christological formula intends to be a safeguard and a development of these definitions, and thus this definition is presupposed as being vitally present.

5. The Finishing Touch: Constantinople (680-681)

And yet this lacuna in the definition of Chalcedon still calls for the supplement which was presented in the struggle against Monotheletism in the seventh century. It is impossible and unnecesary to sketch the controversy surrounding Chalcedon in the following centuries. Large groups of Cyril's disciples continued to reject the "two natures" of Chalcedon as being in conflict with Cyril's **Anathemas**. Monophysitism was especially powerful in Egypt and Syria. A sincere longing for Christian unity as well as the political necessity to restore peace precisely in these threatened provinces repeatedly brought the emperors and the patriarchs of Constantinople to attempt various efforts

at reconciliation and even, if necessary, to accept a
partial relinquishment of Chalcedon. The plan of
Emperor Heraclius (610-641) and Patriach Sergius
(610-638) to restore unity on the basis of a new
creedal formula belongs among these efforts. In the
definition which they planned to legislate as binding
for the Christians of the empire, they forbade from
that time on any mention of "one or two operations,"
since "one and the same only begotten Son our Lord
Jesus Christ has operated the divine as well as the
human" (**Mansi** X. 993Ef.) For, as they say, although
the Fathers speak of one operation, some are scandal-
ized at this. But it is also dangerous to speak of two
operations, because from this it could follow that
there are two opposed wills in the Lord (996AB).

> Therefore . . . we confess one will in our
> Lord Jesus Christ the true God, since the
> rationally animated flesh has never exercised
> only its own natural movement and out of its
> own impulse and in opposition with the good
> pleasure of the . . . God-Word, but only when
> and as and insofar as the God-Word willed".
> (996C).

With this text Monotheletism was born. When
they only intended to express that Jesus' human freedom is continually an act of the one divine Son and
thus inspired by his divine will, their proposition
was not unorthodox and they could truly build a

bridge to the many Monophysites who in their opposition to Chalcedon had precisely this in view.[65] Therefore the fact that Pope Honorius did not originally oppose this is excusable (**DS** 487).

But the best orthodox theologians of the period, Sophronius of Jerusalem (d. 638) and Maximus the Confessor (d. 662), recognized the betrayal of Chalcedon which lurked in the formula of the "one will." At a major Roman Synod (649), which profited from Maximus' superior knowledge of patristic Christology, Pope Martin condemned the teaching of "one operation and one will" in Christ and defined:

> two wills (and operations) of one and the same Christ our God, the divine and the human, which are harmoniously united, since our Redeemer is gifted according to each of his natures with a free will . . . (**DS** 510),

so that a "God-manly operation" can be spoken of in the sense of a genuine twofoldness of divine and human operation (**DS** 515). This definition intends to be nothing other than a further working out of the doctrine of Chalcedon: if Christ is genuinely and fully man, he necessarily possesses a human will and operation (Encyclical of Martin I, [**Mansi** X. 1171BD]). Martin remains entirely within the formal framework of the definition of Chalcedon and does not further reflect on the function of Christ's human willing and acting in the work of salvation.

The perspective was broadened when, thirty years later, Emperor Constantine IV (668-685) summoned a general Council at Constantinople. In preparation, Pope Agatho (678-681) gathered a Council of the Latin Church in Rome, where the Council Fathers risked describing the dogma of Chalcedon in their own words and where the words of Leo's **Tomus** pertaining to the operation of the Word and of the flesh were taken up:

> For out of both natures he is one and each (nature) exists through the One, because the loftiness of the divinity and the littleness of the flesh coalesce. Indeed after the union each nature preserves its property and "each form realizes what is proper to it in community with the other: the Word works what is proper to the Word, and the flesh accomplishes what is proper to the flesh. The one radiates in miracles, the other succumbs under acts of violence." Consequently our orthodox faith teaches us that just as he has two natures or substances . . . , so also he has two natural wills and two natural operations, because indeed one and the same Lord Jesus Christ is fully God and fully man . . . (**DS** 548).

So as we saw in the late Cyril and in the **Tomus** of Leo, there is not simply further discussion of the

formal problem of one person and two natures, but
attention is also directed to the concrete **gestalt** of
the historical Jesus, who shows himself to be God
in his miracles and in his weaknesses to be man,
but who nonetheless is one and the same in both so
that the humanity truly cooperates in his miracles
and the power of God reveals itself in the weakness
of the man.

The Third Council of Constantinople (680-681)
likewise incorporated the quotation from Leo in its
lengthy definition. But at the same time it corrected
a shortcoming inherent in Leo's formulation, which
was a major objection on the part of the Monophysites against Leo and against Chalcedon.[66] In his
rhetorical preference for symmetrical formulae, Leo
had said that the "Word works what is proper to the
Word, and the flesh accomplishes what is proper to
the flesh." But this symmetry is misleading: in the
first clause the personal subject (the Word) is mentioned; in the second, the concrete human nature
(the flesh) is mentioned. But this symmetrical formulation gives the impression that the "flesh" regulates
the human activities as an independent subject. It
is not made sufficiently clear in Leo's formulation
that the Person of the Word is the subject which
also operates in the weakness of the flesh and in
Jesus' human willing and operations. The Council felt

it necessary to clarify this point by further examining
the relationship of Christ's human will to his divine
will (the Council did not speak about the reverse
relationship).

After having literally repeated the definition of
Chalcedon, the Council continued:

> We also proclaim that there are in him
> two natural wills and two natural operations,
> without change, without division, without con-
> fusion. . . .

> And the two natural wills are not in opposi-
> tion . . . , but his human will follows his divine
> and almighty will and subjects itself to it and
> does not set itself in resistance to or struggle
> against it. For the will of the flesh had to be
> moved, but in such a way that it subjected
> itself to the divine will. . . . For as his flesh
> is called and is the flesh of the God-Word, so
> also the natural will of the flesh is called and
> is also the will of the God-Word himself. In
> agreement with what he himself says: "I came
> down out of heaven, not to do my own will,
> but the will of the Father who sent me," in
> which he calls the will of the flesh his own
> will because indeed the flesh has also become
> his own flesh.

> For as his . . . animated flesh was not vio-
> lated by the divinization but remained in its
> own nature, so also his human will was not

> violated by the divinization but on the con-
> trary was preserved. As Gregory the Theolo-
> gian says: "The will which we see in the Re-
> deemer is not in opposition to God, but totally
> divinized" (**DS** 556).

Here the apparent symmetry of Leo's formula
"each form accomplishes what is proper to it, in
community with the other" is refined. This expression
remains completely true, but this "community with
the other" means something different for the divine
and for the human nature. The divine in Christ is
the self-giving and the re-creating, the human is
the receiving and the accepting. Community with
the other nature means for the divine that it empties
itself and imprints itself in the form of man so that
this becomes the expression of the divine Son himself.
But for the human, this community means divinization, through which the human freedom is thoroughly
ablaze with divine resoluteness, as we saw in Cyril.
For this human freedom is truly the freedom of the
Son of God himself, who expressed his absolute
sanctity and love in the act of this earthly flesh.

Or, stated in another way: the definition of Constantinople warns against a possible misinterpretation
of Chalcedon's "one person in two natures." For
this "one person" is in one way identical with his
divine nature, which he is from eternity, and in

another way with his human nature, which he became out of grace "for us and for our salvation."
It is actually only in this definition of Constantinople
that what Chalcedon meant by the teaching that the
one Person of the God-man is no other than the
second Person of the Trinity is realized. It is this
Person, not another, who is himself and realizes himself in the human existence and the human freedom
of Jesus of Nazareth. Thanks to the two centuries
of the theologians wrestling with Monophysitism in
this development of the doctrine of Chalcedon,
termed the "Neo-Chalcedon direction,"[67] the teaching
of Athanasius and of the mature Cyril comes to full
bloom. For Jesus' humanity is divinized because it
is the self-expression of the eternal Son.

A human nature which is divinized is not for this
reason any less truly human. In spite of (or better:
thanks to) the divinization of his humanity, the fact
remains that he "is of one nature with us." The
proper and authentic property of Jesus' soul and body,
of his freedom and his activities, is not violated by
the divinization, but, on the contrary, preserved (the
Greek word can also be translated as "saved," but
since the term in the christological tradition, for
example in Chalcedon, is also used in reference to
the divinity, this translation would be out of place
here).

Divinization makes the human perfectly human. This christological principle, implicit in Chalcedon and explicated in Constantinople, contains the basic foundation of two fundamental propositions of the doctrine of grace. In the first place, that "grace does not destroy nature, but perfects it," that is makes it more itself. And second, that human freedom is not violated by the fact that God's graceful self-sharing takes possession of this freedom: "Freedom should be defined as a faculty of reception, the response to a divine call. . . . The very fact that the (human) will of Christ . . . always acts in union with the divine will . . . constitutes its very freedom."[68]

CONCLUSION

With the Third Ecumenical Council of Constantinople, the period of the great christological definitions is closed and the clarification of the Christ-mystery is in a certain sense brought to completion.

This is not as though this mystery becomes any the less mysterious or impenetrable. It remains the unfathomable abyss of the love of the Father, who, in order to bring man to his own home, had his Son become man in the race of Adam and in the world marked by sin and death. Also the mystery of the "how" of the incarnation and of the constitution of the God-man remains just as dark, in unapproachable light.

Indeed the explication which was brought about by the highest teaching authority of the Church, and due to the intellectual and loving dedication of numerous of her sons and teachers over a period of five centuries, for a large part consisted in the fact that every easy and simple solution was ruled out. A simple solution was that of Arianism which wanted to see in the Son who became man a lofty heavenly being but no true God. Easy also was the answer of Apollinaris, for whom the Word himself was the

animating principle of this human body. Easy was
the solution of Nestorianism, as though everything
was said in stating that in this man the divine Son
dwelt in an eminent manner. Easy also was Monotheletism, which allowed the human freedom of the
Lord to be absorbed in the holiness of God.

The answer of the Church to these errors consisted
in the fact that she preserved the tension of the
opposite poles in its full strength. The unity of the
God-man is more intimate, the proper character of
both the divine and the human is more weighty.
The Son, who becomes man and suffers and dies
and rises, is truly God, of one nature with the eternal
Father (Nicaea). But at the same time he is fully
and completely man, of one nature with us children
of Adam, of whose family he is born and whose life
and death he shares (Constantinople I; Chalcedon).
And in spite of the irreducible difference between
his divine and his human nature, he is one and the
same, the eternal Son of God himself, who as man
is born of Mary the Virgin and Mother of God
(Ephesus; Chalcedon). And that this Son of God
becomes and is man, means that he himself leads
a truly human life, in all aspects like ours except in
sin: a life of truly human actions, of truly human
freedom, of truly human consciousness (Constantinople
III).

With this last definition the development of the christological dogma is in a certain sense rounded off. After the divine majesty of the eternal Son was first preserved at Nicaea, now his human likeness comes into its full rights. For the human life of Jesus of Nazareth is truly the life of the Son of God, who thus has truly shared our human experience of life. And with this comes, in principle, the rounding off of the tension of the two lines of thought which from the New Testament on determine the Christ-image: God who reveals himself in human form; the man who fulfills all justice. Chalcedon had already defined that being-God and being-human coalesce in Jesus. The Council of Constantinople penetrates somewhat deeper into their relationship with one another. Namely, by clarifying that Jesus' human willing is in perfect harmony with his divine will because the human will is also the will of the divine Son himself, the Council makes it clear that Jesus' human activities are a self-relevation of the Son (and thus of the Father). Each human action is indeed an expression of the freedom and thus an expression of the innermost center of the person, of the deepest **bei-sich-sein** and **sich-sein.** But the human freedom which expresses itself in Jesus' human activities is the freedom of the Son himself. This self thus finds its expression in the human activities of the Lord. The Alexandrian school, following the example of

John, has already defended this: the historical form of Jesus of Nazareth is the form of the eternal Son of God himself. This self appears in this form so that we can see and touch him in his twofold involvement: the economic involvement for us and our salvation by which he empties himself totally for us in the gesture of the opened and self-emptying heart; the trinitarian involvement by which he is totally directed to the Father because he is nothing other than a divine "Yes, Father."

But this man, who is nothing other than the form of the Son, is truly and fully man. In obedience to God and in solidarity with his brothers, he has lived and experienced our human life with its suffering and its joys, its loneliness and death, and the eternal surprise of reborn life. Complete and uncurtailed man—the perfect man. The model who shows us the true way; the firstling in whom is realized that for which we may hope; the true man of whose fullness we receive.

We may add to this: he is this perfect man because he is the man in whose voluntary activities and suffering the divine Son expresses himself: because he thus gives himself totally to his fellow men, and in the abandonment of death and in the amazement of the resurrection utters his "Yes, Father" with all his being. Here again the old question of why precisely it was the Son who had to become man becomes clear. This is the question which was asked by Irenaeus but which in the wearying debates about the relationship between the divine (not the filial) and the human in the God-man fell into the background. Because the truth of the human essence is that man recognizes and accepts God as his source, that divine Person had to become man who in the intra-trinitarian life is the recognition and acceptance of God as his source: another Person cannot express himself in a relationship of human dependence. Or, to state the same thing in patristic terminology: the image of God which man is can only be perfected when he who is the eternal Image of the Father expresses himself therein. But in this, man, as image of God, thus also finds his absolute fulfillment.

This dogma presents inexhaustible material for wonder and reflection. It throws light on the nature of our God, who can become man without doing violence to his divinity. Likewise it throws light on the nature of man who becomes perfectly himself due to the fact that the Son expresses himself in him. In addition to the analysis of concepts such as "person" and "nature," theology must also reflect upon these more fundamental questions. But possibly the most important mission which the great christological definitions of the early period present to the future is the completion of the movement first shown by the Third Council of Constantinople which, beginning with the insight into the constitution of the God-man, came to reflect on his work of salvation. In seven centuries of reflection there had grown out of Christ's saving work an insight into who and what he is; now this insight will have to lead in reverse to a deeper understanding of what he has done for us.

NOTES

1. A Gilg, *Weg und Bedeutung der altkirchlichen Christologie* (München, 1955), p. 7.

2. A. Grillmeier, *Vom Symbolum zur Summa,* in *Kirche und Ueberlieferung,* Festschrift J. R. Geiselmann (Freiburg, 1960), pp. 160-164.

3. A. Grillmeier, S.J. and H. Bacht, S.J., *Das Konzil von Chalkedon, Geschichte und Gegenwart* (Würtzburg, 1951-1954), especially in the first article: A. Grillmeier, *Die theologische und sprachliche Vorbereitung der christologischen Formel von Chalkedon,* I, pp. 5-202. Grillmeier excludes from his study the connection between Christology and soteriology with the result that his remarkable study especially concentrates on the formal aspects of Christology.

See also A. Grillmeier, S.J. *Christ in Christian Tradition.* Translated by J. S. Bowden (London: A. R. Mowbray and Co., 1965; New York: Sheed & Ward, 1965). The references in P. Smulders' work are to the German writings of Grillmeier.

Strongly dependent upon Grillmeier is the outstanding overview in: J. N. D. Kelly, *Early Christian Doctrines* (London, 1958).

A rich collection of patristic material is offered in B. M. Xiberta, O.Carm., *Enchiridion de Verbo Incarnato* (Matriti, 1957).

4. A Grillmeier, *op. cit.,* p. 131: "die theologische Leistung der Vater (ist) zu sehen in der . . . Zusammenschau von 'Oikonomia' und 'Theologia.' . . . Dieser 'okonomische' Bezug der 'Theologie' und die 'theologische' Tiefe der 'Oikonomia,' die Einheit zudem von kosmolohischer Schau und geschicht-

licher Betrachtung machen die Grosse des frühchristlichen
Entwurfes der Glaubenslehre aus."

5. For Irenaeus, *puer* calls up the idea of an intra-
trinitarian obedience of the Son toward the Father: A.
Houssiau, *La Christologie de saint Irénée* (Louvain, 1955),
p. 35: "L'Epideixis comprend 'pais mou' d'Isaie XLIX, 6
dans le sens de 'serviteur,' et l'applique au Fils préexistant.
Le titre convient au Fils en raison de l'obéissance inhérente
à sa condition de Fils."

6. This passage is later imitated by Gregory the Great,
Bede, and others.

7. The theory is borrowed from Tertullian, *De Resur-
rectione Mortuorum* 51/2, CC II, p. 944 (below p. 12), where
arrabon is also connected with the mediator text.

8. H. E. W. Turner, *The Patristic Doctrine of Redemption*
(London, 1952), pp. 103f.

9. "sürnenden Gott, der versohnt werden muss" (A. von
Harnack, *Lehrbuch der Dogmengeschichte,* 4II. p. 180).

10. The authenticity of this work is contested, but it is
certain that it comes from the time of Cyprian.

11. Ch. Bigg, *The Christian Platonists of Alexandria*
(²1913), p. 104, n. 1.

12. Cf. F. Bertrand, *Mystique de Jésus chez Origène*
(1951), pp. 15ff.

13. "Connaitre pour Origène, c'est 'etre semblable,'
's'unir' " (P. Nemeshegyi, *La paternité de Dieu chez Origène*
[Doornik, 1960], p. 168).

14. H. Crouzel, *Théologie de l'image de Dieu chez Origène*
(Paris, 1956), pp. 135-142.

15. Cf. Nemeshegyi, *op. cit.,* pp. 93-95.

16. "die so begründete Einheit in Christus (ist) als eine
wirklich *ontische* Einheit gemeint" (Grillmeier, *Vorbereitung
der Formel von Chalkedon,* p. 65).

16a. *De Princip.* II. 6, 6; cf. *Matt. Comm. Ser. 65, GCS* 38, p. 152; "substantiae proprietatem."

17. "de considérer l'image comme une copie dégradée et affaiblie du modèle" (Crouzel, *op. cit.,* p. 45).

18. Cf. H. U. von Balthasar, *Parole et mystère chez Origène* (Paris, 1957), pp. 18f.

19. Cf. M. Harl, *Origène et la fonction revélatrice du Verbe incarné* (Paris, 1958), pp. 197f.

20. G. Wingren, *Man and the Incarnation: a Study in the Biblical Theology of Irenaeus* (Edinburgh, 1959), p. 212.

21. *Les actes du procès de Paul de Samosate* (Fribourg, 1952); in the following we will refer to the collection of fragments (fr.) contained in this work.

22. *Brief der zes Bisschoppen,* in A. Hahn, *Bibliothek der Symbole* (³1897), p. 173.

23. In Hahn, *op. cit.,* pp. 181f.

24. De Riedmatten, *op. cit.,* pp. 57f.

25. De Riedmatten, *op. cit.,* pp. 70-81; H. Berkhof, *Die Theologie des Eusebius von Caesarea* (Amsterdam, 1939), p. 120.

26. See Grillmeier, *op. cit.,* pp. 68-73.

27. "De tout etre spirituel qui s'emprisonne dane un corps on pourra dire qu'il 'devient homme,' puisqu'il se trouve etre un esprit incarné" (J. Liebaert, *La doctrine christologique de saint Cyrille d'Alexandrie avant la querelle nestorienne* [Lille, 1951], p. 148).

28. In opposition to Liebaert is, for example, H. M. Diepen, *Aux origines de l'anthropologie de saint Cyrille d'Alexandrie* (Brugge, 1957): the bibliography of this question is enormous and out of all proportion to its true importance.

29. Grillmeier, *op. cit.,* p. 74, n. 3; p. 76, n. 9.

30. See above, p. 64.

31. Letter of Arius to Eusebius, ed. H. Opitz, *Athanasius Werke*, Urk. 1, 4-5 pp. 2-3; cf. Arius' profession of faith directed to his bishop, Alexander, Urk. 6, 2-4 p. 12.

32. We translate *homoousios* as "of one nature" because the ordinary translation "of one substance" can in a sense be misleading. At the time of Nicaea, namely, this word did not yet signify the one divine substance which, undivided and identical, is the Father and the Son. The word was still connected with an older usage in which it meant, more or less, "of the same stuff" (*van dezelfde grondstof*), of the same dough. When used of the Son then it expressed that he is truly of divine "stuff," of the same strictly divine nature as the Father.

33. Turner, *op. cit.*, p. 87.

34. Both translated by Th. Camelot in *Sources Chrétiennes* 18 (1947); the last translated by H. Berkhof, in *Klassieken der Kerk* 4 (1949).

35. Translation by C. de Vogel in *Monumenta Christiana* II, p. 197; cf. n. 70, p. 198; *De Synodis* 51.

36. Other texts in de Vogel, *op. cit.*, p. XXXIX.

37. Grillmeier, *op. cit.*, pp. 91-97.

38. Also in n. 2 of this letter we find an argument against a proposition of Apollinaris, namely, that Jesus' body is *homoousios* with the Godhead: cf. Apollin. fragm. 153.

39. *Les actes du procès de Paul de Samosate*, p. 53; cf. H. de Riedmatten, *La christologie d'Apollinaire de Laodicée* in *Studia Patristica* II, pp. 208-234.

40. Grillmeier, *op. cit.*, p. 116; G. Prestige, *Fathers and Heretics* (1948), p. 107.

41. *Ep. ad Jovianum*, ed. Lietzmann, *Apollinaris von Laodicea und seine Schule* (1904), p. 253; in the following we will refer to the collection of fragments in Lietzmann.

42. Cf. Grillmeier, *op. cit.*, p. 109, n. 6.

43. De Riedmatten, in *Studia Patrist.*, pp. 212f., also cites unpublished exegetical fragments of this same tenor.

44. De Riedmatten, *op. cit.*, p. 218.

45. See p. 75, above.

46. The fragments of Eustathius are collected by M. Spanneut, *Recherches sur les écrits d'Eustathe d'Antioche* (Lille, 1948).

47. F. A. Sullivan, *The Christology of Theodore of Mopsuestia* (Rome, 1956), p. 182.

48. In Sullivan, *op. cit.*, p. 187, n. 65.

49. *Ibid.*, p. 186, n. 61.

50. *Ibid.*, p. 189.

51. In Leontius of Byzantium, *Contra Nest. et Eutych.* III, *PG* 68, 1388C.

52. Sullivan, *op. cit.*, pp. 287f.

53. "si, sans s'exprimer à la manière de saint Cyrille d'Alexandrie, il n'aurait cependant pas reconnu comme lui le Fils de Dieu dans le fils de la Vierge" (P. Galtier, *Théodore de Mopsueste:sa vraie pensée sur l'Incarnation,* in: *Rech. Sc. Rel.* 45 [1957], 161-186, 338-360; the quote is on p. 161).

54. *Les Homélies Catéchétiques de Théodore de Mopsueste,* translated by Tonneau-Devreesse (Vaticano, 1949).

55. Theodore's opponents understood this to be the disposition of the man; but this is certainly not his intention.

56. See above, p. 90.

57. See above pp. 91ff.

58. Grillmeier, *op. cit.*, p. 189.

59. Sullivan, *op. cit.*, p. 204.

60. See, for example, Grillmeier, *op. cit.*, pp. 165-182; H. du Manoir de Juaye, *Dogme et spiritualité chez S. Cyrille d'Alexandrie* (Paris, 1943), pp. 114-143.

61. Cf. du Manoir, *op. cit.*, p. 206.

62. C. Verhoeven, *Het Woord Substantia*, in *Tds. v. Philos.* 22 (1960), 512.

63. Cf. I. Ortiz de Urbina, *Das Symbol von Chalkedon*, in: *Das Konzil von Chalkedon* I, pp. 389-418.

64. Thus, for example, Bihlmeyer-Tuchle, *Kirchenge-schichte* I, par. 55, n. 2.

65. Cf. W. Elert, *Der ausgang der altkirchlichen Christ-ologie* (Berlin, 1957), p. 152.

66. W. Elert, *loc. cit.*

67. Ch. Moeller, *Le chalcédonisme et le néo-chalcédonisme en Orient*, in *Das Konzil von Chalkedon* I, pp. 637-720.

68. "La liberté doit se définir une faculté d'accueil, de réponse à un appel divin. . . . Le fait meme que la volonté (humaine) du Christ . . . agit toujours en union avec la volonté divine . . . constitue sa liberté meme" (Moeller, *op. cit.*, p. 714).